Yuwipi

No vision in the heavens came to me.
I saw the mountains yonder gleaming tall,
And clouds that burned with evening. That was all.

But while the Holy One was praying there,

I felt a strangeness growing in the air
As when, a boy, I wakened in the night,
And there was something!

John G. Neihardt,
"The Song of the Messiah"

Yuwipi

Vision and Experience in Oglala Ritual

by
William K. Powers

University of Nebraska Press: Lincoln and London

The paper in this book meets the guidelines for permanence and durability of the Committee on Production Guidelines for Book Longevity of the Council on Library Resources.

Library of Congress Cataloging in Publication Data

Powers, William K.
  Yuwipi, vision and experience in Oglala ritual.

  Bibliography: p.
  Includes index.
  1. Oglala Indians—Religion and mythology. 2. Oglala Indians—Rites and ceremonies. 3. Indians of North America—Great Plains—Religion and mythology. 4. Indians of North America—Great Plains—Rites and ceremonies. I. Title.
E99.Q3P683   299'.74   81-10501
ISBN 0-8032-3663-8   AACR2

To my mother and father

Contents

Preface

> Whether the myth is recreated by the individual or borrowed from tradition, it derives from its sources—individual or collective (between which interpenetrations and exchanges constantly occur)—only the stock of representations with which it operates. But the structure remains the same, and through it the symbolic function is fulfilled.
>
> [Lévi-Strauss 1963:199]

In an earlier work, *Oglala Religion* (1977), I focused on the structural and symbolic relationships among several Oglala (Sioux) cultural domains—myth, ritual, social organization, and so forth. In this book my task is to explain similar relationships between three Oglala rituals—the vision quest, the sweat lodge, and Yuwipi (pronounced yoo-WEE-pee), a modern curing ritual. At first I had planned to present only the last ritual, which is less well known than the others, offering the first complete translation of Yuwipi to help the reader understand what it is like to experience this important contemporary ritual. But as the writing progressed I found it necessary to include the first two because the three together exhibit a particular relationship not necessarily found among other rituals. My selection of these three is not arbitrary. The vision quest and sweat lodge have a particular status among the Oglalas: they are regarded as the oldest, the "original" rituals that existed before the arrival of the White Buffalo Calf Maiden and her gifts of the sacred pipe and sacred rites.

There is also a structural relationship between these two rituals. Although a sweat lodge may be conducted independently of any other rituals, for both spiritual and salutary reasons it also serves as a preparatory and concluding ritual for the vision quest. The two contrast, then, in that the sweat lodge can be an independent ritual, whereas the vision quest is partially dependent on the sweat lodge to achieve full efficacy.

A similar relationship exists between the sweat lodge and Yuwipi, but not always after it. This is an ideal relationship, and there are variations. For example, when it is necessary to conduct an "emergency" Yuwipi, the formality of holding a sweat lodge is often dispensed with. On the other hand, Yuwipis are sometimes conducted serially, usually for four nights, and when this happens a sweat lodge may be conducted each night before the Yuwipi, on alternating nights, or sometimes only before the first night or after the last.

Under certain conditions—when the efficacy of the Yuwipi ritual is enhanced by the simultaneous performance of the vision quest, for both of which the sweat lodge serves as prelude and postlude—the three rituals are interdependent. The relations between these three rituals become obvious if we examine the individuals who participate and the expectations that are important to them. It is only by examining the interrelations and exchanges that we can understand precisely what symbolic functions are fulfilled and to whom the benefits of these rituals accrue.

When the three rituals are performed together, three participants figure prominently: the ritual specialist, who in this context is known as a Yuwipi man; the patient who appeals to the Yuwipi man to cure him; and an individual who pledges to perform the vision quest in an effort to strengthen his own ties with the spiritual world and, by so doing, to help guarantee an effective cure for the patient. The three play out their interrelated roles against the backdrop of the collective, the people of a community who share kinship ties, real or putative. The members of the community participate in the Yuwipi by singing and praying; some of them join in the sweat lodge. But only one, the person who has pledged the vision quest, separates himself and embarks upon this dangerous ordeal atop a sacred hill. A dilemma ensues: to help effect the patient's cure, the pledger must expose himself to danger and accomplish his mission. To ensure his safety, the people must concentrate their prayers not on the patient, but on the pledger; for if either ritual fails the pledger may be harmed by evil spirits, the patient may die, and the ritual specialist may lose his power.

Throughout the book I have attempted to inject a sense of

experientiality into the objective descriptions. After thirty years of research and of participation in the sweat lodge and Yuwipi (but not subjectively in the vision quest), I feel that this personal view will be useful in conveying the way these rituals affect one's sensory perceptions and one's emotions. It is likely that my experience of Oglala ritual will agree with those of some Oglalas but not others. I regard this as a kind of reverse ethnography, in which I can make claims that are ultimately verifiable by the Oglalas as well as by anthropologists and other social scientists. I think it is reasonable to assume not only that all history is written from a particular point of view, one directed to a selected audience, as Lévi-Strauss argues, but that the same claim may be made for ethnography. Just as all history is "history-for" (Lévi-Strauss 1966:245–70), so all ethnography is "ethnography-for." The main point here is that I recognize myself in the ethnography that follows.

I am grateful to the Oglala people of Red Cloud Community, about whom this book is written. Before their deaths, George and Julie Plenty Wolf spent a great deal of time instructing me in the rituals of Yuwipi, the sweat lodge, and the vision quest, and I hope this book faithfully conveys to the reader the same significance that these two marvelous people meant it to.

Additionally, thanks to Basil Plenty Wolf, the late Owen Brings and his wife, Celeste, Mr. and Mrs. Melvin Red Cloud, Mr. and Mrs. William Horn Cloud, Mr. and Mrs. Oliver Red Cloud, Mrs. Zona Fills the Pipe, Mr. and Mrs. Clarence Janis, the late Mrs. Alice Red Cloud, Mrs. Charlotte Ortiz, Mr. and Mrs. Ellis Chips, Royal Bull Bear, Mr. and Mrs. Henry White Calf, Mr. and Mrs. Richard Elk Boy, Mr. and Mrs. Edgar Red Cloud, Mr. and Mrs. Francis Brown, the late Joe Shakes Spear, Mark Big Road, the late Levi Fast Horse, the late Howard Blue Bird, and Mrs. Agnes Lamont.

I owe a special thanks to the Reverend Paul B. Steinmetz, S.J., who was kind enough to share with me tapes and translations of various rituals, or segments of rituals, that are integrated into this book. I also gratefully acknowledge two grants from the American Philosophical Society in 1966 and 1967 that partly subsidized my travel to Pine Ridge.

As in my other works on the Oglalas, I assume full responsibility for what follows.

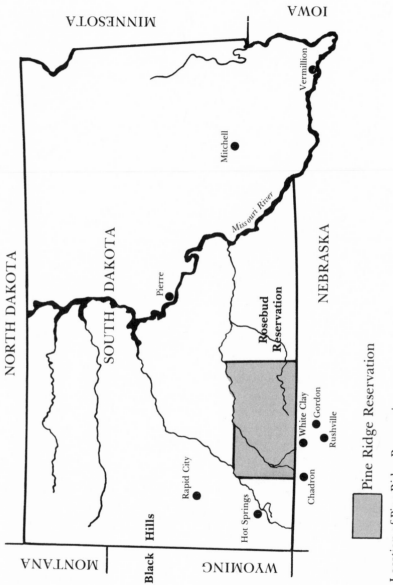

MINNESOTA

IOWA

Vermillion

Mitchell

Missouri River

NORTH DAKOTA

SOUTH DAKOTA

Pierre

NEBRASKA

Rosebud
Reservation

MONTANA

Black Hills

WYOMING

Rapid City

Hot Springs

Chadron

White Clay
Gordon
Rushville

Pine Ridge Reservation

Location of Pine Ridge Reservation

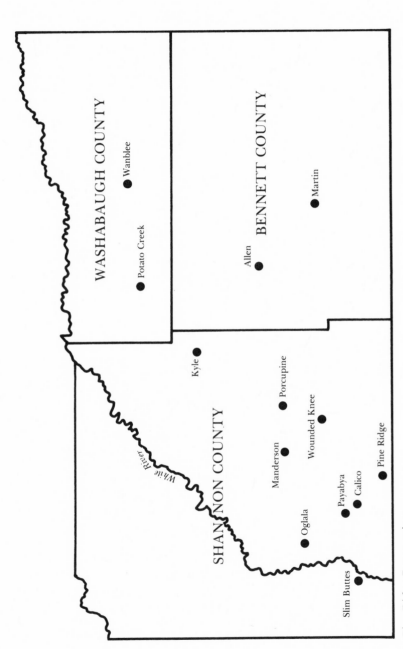

WASHABAUGH COUNTY

Wanblee

Potato Creek

BENNETT COUNTY

Martin

Allen

Kyle

Porcupine

Wounded Knee

Manderson

SHANNON COUNTY

White River

Pine Ridge

Payabya

Calico

Oglala

Slim Buttes

Pine Ridge Reservation

Introduction

One of the essential problems any anthropologist meets in the field is the often arbitrary and random way he must collect his data. In entering the field he creates his own "beginning," so to speak, for a cultural story that has been going on since long before he arrived. Similarly, his ethnography "ends" when he leaves, though the culture continues (usually very well) without him. His entry and exit, then, become contextual delineators, and everything he selects to observe between these two temporal markers becomes the subject of his ethnography.

As both participant and observer, the anthropologist plays a dual role. As a collector of ethnographic data, he is like a cinematographer who has been directed to shoot a number of disparate scenes for a motion picture. Many factors influence just how the scenes will be shot—time of day or night, appropriateness of the weather, readiness of the properties, costumes, and actors—all, or at least many of them, matters tied to the film budget. Thus a cinematographer may shoot scenes, just as the anthropologist collects facts, in a random, often haphazard way relative to the final production.

Once the facts have been collected, however (or the film has been shot), it is necessary to put the data (or film takes) into some meaningful order. At this point the anthropologist's role becomes more analogous to that of a film editor who, after collecting thousands of feet of film, must, in collaboration with the director, splice sections together in a sequence that has some meaning when projected on the screen. In the final film, first things happen first, last things happen last; plot, actors, and actions fit together in time and space in a way that makes sense to an audience.

The final result of the motion picture or the ethnography, then, is an illusion of sorts: it did not really happen that way—not the way the finished product suggests. Yet both the film and the ethnography can be critically evaluated or tested against a wider reality. It is the audience viewing the film that confirms its validity. But in the case of the ethnography the verification of reality can come only from the people whose cultural actions it describes.

Anthropological analysis, on the other hand, when it can be distinguished from ethnographic description, is the way anthropologists test hypotheses. It is performed for the members of the anthropologist's culture, either specialists or nonspecialists. What the analysis does, then, is to explain the culture of one group of people from the point of view of another culture.

When the anthropologist's analysis is largely a matter of description, of organizing ethnographic observations in some meaningful way, the only valid criticism must come from the natives themselves, because they are the only ones capable of determining whether the data the anthropologist has collected are significant to them and properly arranged. Although at one time this was impossible, because anthropologists worked in nonliterate societies, today many societies that are subjects of anthropological research are literate, and scholars from these societies are capable of making critical evaluations of an outsider's impression of their culture. This is not without problems, however, problems that have to do with consensus about what observations are culturally valid. Cultural validity thus becomes a problem for the native critic, just as theoretical soundness becomes an issue for the anthropologist's colleagues. What is important in the first case is whether the ethnography elicits from native critics an evaluation that is statistically measurable in native society. What I mean is this. Not all members of one culture necessarily share all the behaviors available to that culture; there may be religious differences, economic distinctions, political disagreements. But within a given society there will be a general agreement on whether a particular range of behavior is culturally feasible.

If the anthropologist is capable of successfully collecting social facts and native evaluations of those facts, and if he is capable of organizing them in a manner meaningful to the native, then it can be said that he has learned some rules of behavior appropriate to the culture he has undertaken to study. Now the ethnographer has cut to the heart of his study and is pursuing the ultimate objective of anthropology, which is like the goal of the linguist who seeks not simply to record a language, but to speak it.

This leads me to my choice of a narrative exposition of the sweat lodge, vision quest, and Yuwipi. I have tried to organize the ethnography of the three rituals into a meaningful sequence, taking into consideration not only what is observable to me, but, perhaps most important, why the characters involved in all three rituals are motivated to behave as they do. Like the film-maker, I have collected my data out of sequence, and here I want to make it clear just how this came about.

First, all the characters described in the rituals are real people, some living, some dead. I have changed the names of only two, the character Runs Again, who in the ritual is identified as the patient, and his son Wayne. I have also changed the kinship terms shared by the ritual specialist Plenty Wolf and his undifferentiated "nephew." These changes have been made to protect these characters' privacy, but under different names and in different circumstances they have really existed. All the other characters' names remain unchanged because they have agreed to it. Furthermore, many of them have been cited in previous literature on Oglala ritual, and my including them in this book betokens my highest respect and acknowledges a lifetime of friendship with them.

To what extent I have "participated" or "observed" is best explained systematically, so that the reader will understand how the ethnographic organization came about.

The chapter "Sacred Stones" is based on interviews with Oglala people who are regular participants in traditional rituals, and in each case where a rationale is offered for a specific ritual behavior the rationale is based on Oglala concepts rather than on those from Western intellectual tradition. The rationale by which Runs Again and his son decide to sponsor the Yuwipi is garnered from interviews and from the recordings of the entire three rituals, one of which I did not attend.

Both chapters on the vision quest, "On the Hill" and "Off the Hill," are based on my own observations of the sacred place and on interviews with Plenty Wolf and other Oglala men who were placed on the hill by Plenty Wolf. The actual vision is a composite, since revealing the nature of vision quests is frowned upon by the Oglalas today. It is rare that one can collect this kind of information, though it is not impossible.

Both chapters on the sweat lodge, "Inside" and "Outside," are based on my own participation inside the sweat lodge as well as on my serving as the fire tender at other sweat lodges. Once, as fire tender, I tape-recorded the sweat lodge from the outside with the permission of Plenty Wolf and the other participants.

The middle chapters, dealing with the preparation of the Yuwipi meeting place, the curing ritual, and the feast, are based on my own participation in several rituals, as well as on tape recordings I and others made inside the Yuwipi meeting with the permission of Plenty Wolf.

All the tapes were recorded in the native language, which I have translated. Again, the songs used in all three rituals were translated from the tapes of the sweat lodge and Yuwipis, and they were also collected independent of their ritual context, where I was able to spend some time with the singers learning to understand their meanings. Likewise, Plenty Wolf's "vision talk," a public recital of his own vision quests, was taped by him independent of the Yuwipi meetings because the words were not clearly enunciated on the tapes made during the actual meeting.

With the exception of two vision texts that I collected in 1971 and 1976, all the data were gathered during the summers of 1966 and 1967, when I had the great opportunity of working closely with Plenty Wolf and the various people of Red Cloud Community. The entire ethnography of ritual is based on my own fieldwork, some of which has appeared in other publications. In order to maintain an even flow through the ethnography, I have not cited my own work.

An
Anthropological
View

Black Gown, if you will promise to give me three blankets, I will allow you to tie me with ropes as you may think proper. In your presence I will invoke my spirits, they will loose your ropes, and you will see me here as free as I am now.

Anonymous [Wallis 1947:103]

Yuwipi has always existed in part as a polemic against the threat of intrusive religious and political systems. The quotation above is attributed to an anonymous medicine man who thus challenged the efficacy of Father A. Ravoux, a Jesuit who lived among the Sisseton at Mendota, Minnesota, during the winter of 1843–44. About this medicine man, Ravoux states:

> The old man appeared to be much frightened, and to induce me to believe him, he related to me the following anecdote: "Once when invoking my spirits with solemnity, in a tepee prepared for that purpose, they raised me up, and then irritated against me they let me fall down, and I was almost killed." Placing then his right hand on his face, and showing me a large scar he had on one of his cheeks, he told me that that would give me an idea of the wound, and that it was wrong to show any disrespect to the spirits, because they might become very much irritated and cause us great evils. Whether the statement was true or not, I am convinced that some of the Indians have communication with the evil spirits, and through them may perform wonderful works. [Wallis 1947:103]

The attitudes expressed here by both medicine man and priest had not substantially changed when I first arrived at Pine Ridge in 1948. I stayed at Holy Rosary Mission under the kind auspices of the late Father Gerald Fuller, S.J., and it is there I was first told about the ability of the "devil" to work wonders at Yuwipis, or "spirit meetings" as they were then called in English. It may be partially owing to this long historical criticism of Yuwipi-like rituals by the Jesuits and other ecclesiastics that the phenomenon was able to escape the literature until 1946. Although the Oglalas have always considered Yuwipi to be "very old," it was not until that year that Macgregor identified it as "the only continuing cult of the old Dakota religion," a cult that "worships manifestations of four chief Dakota gods and invokes supernatural power for curing sick and occasionally for finding lost articles" (1946:98–99).

If we look at some of the diagnostic features of present-day Yuwipi, particularly binding the medicine man, conducting the ritual in a darkened room, and invoking spirits and sacred stones to help cure patients or find lost articles, then certainly Yuwipi-like rituals or, as they are technically known in anthropology, "shamanic cult institutions" (Wallace 1966), are widespread throughout sub-arctic North America, from Siberia to the Atlantic seaboard, south to where similar rituals seem to flourish around the Great Lakes. Densmore mentions the practice of tying the medicine man and the use of sacred stones for finding lost objects among the Ojibwas (1910), Menominis (1932), and Tetons, but not the Oglalas (1918). Lynd (1864) and Fletcher (1884) make similar observations for other Siouan peoples, as does Wallis (1947) for the Canadian Dakotas. Buechel's field notes from about 1900 refer to certain Lakota terms used to describe Yuwipi phenomena, but his work was not published until 1970. Deloria's interviews, not published, discuss Yuwipi, but only in the native language (Deloria, n.d.). Although the characteristic traits of Yuwipi have existed for at least 150 years, there are still problems with understanding why the term itself has emerged only recently.

Nearly all previous ethnographers translate Yuwipi as "to wrap," or "they wrap him up," focusing on what has often been regarded as the most salient feature of the ritual, the Yuwipi man's being wrapped in a blanket or quilt and firmly bound (Hurt and Howard 1952; Ruby 1955; Hurt 1960; Feraca 1961, 1962, 1963; Fugle 1966; and Kemnitzer 1968, 1970, 1976). Yuwipi is derived from *yuwi*, which Riggs glosses "to wrap around, bind up, bandage"

(Buechel 1970:656; Riggs 1890:646). Buechel also refers to "yuwipi—transparent stones, usually found on ant hills and used in the *wakan wicoȟ'an* called yuwipi, which consists of one being tied all around and being loosed by magic"; and "yuwipi wasicun—a sacred round hard stone that is supposed to have power in the hands of those who have dreamed" (Buechel 1970:656).

There seems to be some disagreement among Oglala respondents about the precise derivation of the term. In 1950 Henry White Calf, a prominent singer from Loafer Camp, defined Yuwipi for me in the following way:

> Yuwipi means to roll up something like a ball of yarn. In the meetings they roll up that string [of tobacco offerings used to delineate the altar], and it looks like a ball of yarn or string. That's why they call it Yuwipi.

In 1966 George Plenty Wolf, a Yuwipi man from Red Cloud Community, told me that the actual "wrapping" of the medicine man is called *wicapaȟtapi* 'they bind them,' while the untying is called *wicayujujupi* 'they untie them.' Plenty Wolf agreed with White Calf that the rolling up of the tobacco offerings and ropes used to bind the medicine man were properly "yuwipi," and the disagreement may lie in the fact that the practice of tying the medicine man is well known even to those who normally do not attend the meetings and thus are not familiar with the subtler but equally meaningful parts of the ritual. Based on the linguistic evidence proffered by White Calf and Plenty Wolf, I tend to opt for their explication. Whereas in English we "wrap" a bandage, a package, or a cloak and "roll" a cigarette, a ball of string or yarn, or a pair of dice, Lakota employs specific verbs to indicate these diverse forms of action, the significances of which are not interchangeable. The verbs *wicapaȟtapi* 'they bind them' and *wicayujujupi* 'they untie them' more precisely denote the actions employed in the treatment of the medicine man. This analysis is in no way critical of the agreement between earlier anthropologists to gloss *yuwipi* as "they wrap them up." This gloss has increasingly become the translation offered by lay Oglalas as well as by Yuwipi men themselves.

If we return to the problem of the term's absence in the literature until 1946, we may take as a starting point Kemnitzer's observations that "after eighty years of suppression and apparent disuse, a ritual of only minor importance in prereservation times is now the focus [of] a revival of traditional religion and syncretism among the Oglala" (Kemnitzer 1970:40). The eighty years of suppression re-

fers to the prohibition placed on Oglala religion by the federal
government in 1883 that outlawed the Sun dance and other important ceremonies. The syncretism to which Kemnitzer refers, if I
understand him correctly, is a process whereby characteristic features of numerous Oglala rituals were conflated into curing rituals
such as Yuwipi. The known fact that Oglala religion was suppressed
by the government makes it understandable that perhaps a
significant part of it went underground. There are good reasons to
believe that what we are witnessing in Yuwipi is not so much a revival
as it is a continuation of a ritual that perhaps was important in
prereservation days but that, along with other aspects of Oglala
belief, submerged to escape the white man's criticism. Its syncretic
features probably evolved as several rituals related to hunting and
warfare became dysfunctional owing to Euro-American dominance.

   It is not particularly important whether Yuwipi as a term is new
or old. What is important is that those ritual specialists who conduct
Yuwipi and Yuwipi-like rituals continue a tradition whose roots lie in
the nebulous past. As I have pointed out elsewhere (Powers 1977),
old values have a way of structuring themselves into newfound
relevance even when their original cultural manifestations have
disintegrated. Yuwipi, then, subsumes not only syncretic features of
traditional Oglala religion, but features of other institutions such as
economics, politics, and sociality.

   All traditions, of course, have some historical point of depar-
ture. But tracing Yuwipi back to that first event is like attempting to
trace one's own clan genealogy back to its totemic founder.

   Although the "totemic" founder is forever lost to us, we may
trace the historical provenance of Yuwipi at least back to a single
medicine man whose mysterious past is on the lips of nearly every
Yuwipi man currently practicing on the Pine Ridge and Rosebud
reservations. His Lakota name was Ptehe Woptuȟ'a, which signifies
a buffalo horn that has somehow been pulverized, like a dry leaf
crumbled in the hand, or hard clay that disintegrates beneath one's
boot. The name itself connotes something mystical, some arcane
event that perhaps will never be known; it is a name appropriate
for a medicine man who is said to have been mentor to Crazy Horse
himself. In English the name loses some of this mystical charm; the
founder is known simply as Horn Chips.

   Horn Chips, also known as Tahunska (His Leggings), was born
in 1836 and died in 1916 (cf. Steinmetz 1980 for a genealogy). He
was a member of Chief Lip's band of Wajajes, Upper Brules who

joined the Oglalas in 1854. Only glimpses of his life are remembered, most of them associating him with Crazy Horse during the turmoil of the 1860's. Judge E. S. Ricker, a resident of Nebraska who served for ten years with the Indian Service, interviewed "Chips" (whom Ricker also calls "Encouraging Bear") in 1906–7 along with other Oglalas who knew Crazy Horse. Chips sets the tone of those old days when he describes how his junior, Crazy Horse, warred against hostile tribes:

> When we were young all we thought about was going to war with some other nation; all tried to get their names up the highest and whoever did so was the principal man in the nation; and Crazy Horse wanted to get to the highest station and rank. [Ricker 1906–7]

Ricker states:

> Before going into battle [Crazy Horse] always threw a handful of dust over himself and his pony and never wore anything more than a breech cloth and leggings, a single hawk feather in his hair, his ever-present small stone behind his ear, and another stone from Chips under his left arm. [Ricker 1906–7]

Eleanor Hinman, in an interview in 1930–31 with the Oglala Red Feather, corroborates Chips's mentorship of Crazy Horse. Red Feather states:

> Nearly every summer for the rest of his life, Crazy Horse went out on war parties against the Crows or Shoshonis. In 1862 or 1863 a medicine man named Chips, a friend of his youth, made him a special charm to ward off danger, a little white stone with a hole through it, suspended from a buckskin string that Crazy Horse wore slung over his shoulder and under his left arm. [Hinman 1930–31]

Apparently Chips had other powers. He was accused of making a love potion enabling Crazy Horse to steal Black Buffalo Woman, the wife of No Water (who later followed the lovers to their camp and shot Crazy Horse in the face, leaving a scar under his left nostril for the rest of his life). But Chips denied it, saying that he had made only a protective charm for Crazy Horse.

The reference to stones here is important, for as we shall see sacred stones play an important part in Oglala ritual and belief. The early chroniclers of Siouan religions make numerous references to the importance of sacred stones in a variety of rituals that predate Yuwipi (see particularly Densmore 1918; Dorsey 1894; Lynd 1864; Pond 1867; and Riggs 1869, 1893). What I think is significant is that the close association between Horn Chips and Crazy Horse identifies the former with particularly strong *protective* and *curative* powers. Since some of Crazy Horse's current popularity rests on his daring as a warrior in prereservation times, at least part of his magical powers are attributed to the *wotawe,* or sacred charms, made for him by Horn Chips. Most Oglalas today not only emphasize the mentor relationship between Horn Chips and Crazy Horse, but likewise claim that the two were relatives (cf. Steinmetz 1980:21–22).

I do not want to give the impression that the Oglalas regard Horn Chips as the "founder" of Yuwipi. Yuwipi is considered to be even older than this distinguished sacred man. But no one to my knowledge, and this is verified in the Yuwipi literature, has been associated so dramatically with early forms of ritual curing as Horn Chips.

More than the historical connection between Horn Chips and Crazy Horse provides a direct link between contemporary Yuwipi and its recent past. Something is known about the nature of Horn Chips's rituals and about the powers that made them efficacious. According to Hassrick, a man named Black Horse had dreamed of thunder and became worried that he would be struck by lightning. He therefore sought the services of the "Heyoka, Horn Chips" who agreed to supervise his vision quest. Hassrick states:

> Before daybreak Horn Chips gave Black Horse a piece of pemmican and a sip of water, and then the four Heyokas escorted Black Horse to the top of Eagle Nest Butte. When they reached the summit the Heyokas cleaned out the vision pit, and covered the hole with an opening to the north, large enough for a man to rest in. This had been used on other occasions by men seeking visions. Now they lined it with a bed of fresh sage. Horn Chips set up sticks with tobacco offerings and colored banners at the four sides. Around the perimeter, enclosing the pit, were strung many tiny tobacco offerings, each tied in a bundle made of a bit of flesh from Black Horse's forearms and thighs, in order to supplicate the supernaturals. [Hassrick 1964:233]

Horn Chips ultimately interpreted Black Horse's vision, saying that Black Horse too would become a *heyoka.*

Hassrick's observations are important because he identifies Horn Chips as a *heyoka* and describes the organization of the vision "pit" and the way it is sanctified. As we shall see later, the form of the vision quest has changed little, if at all. Furthermore, numerous references to *heyoka* spirits appearing at contemporary Yuwipi meetings partly distinguish this form of curing ritual from other Yuwipi-like rituals.

Hassrick's mention of Eagle Nest Butte is also significant. Wanbli Hoňpi, as it is called in Lakota, is a prominent topographic feature of the northeastern part of Pine Ridge Reservation. It is five miles south of the present community of Wanblee and, as the local people tell you, was originally a site for trapping eagles—thus its name. Other prominent buttes nearby are Buzzard Butte, Saddle Butte, and Snake Butte, the last named for its abundant rattlesnake dens. All these buttes are, and have been for as long as the Oglalas can remember, sacred places where generations of Indians have gone on vision quests.

It is in the vicinity of Eagle Nest Butte, and the present community of Wanblee, that Chief Lip's Wajajes settled about 1880. Originally Lip's camp was east of Pass Creek on the Rosebud Reservation. Although they are technically Sicangus, there had been a strong tie between Lip's people and the Oglalas since 1854. In the summer of 1890, the boundary between Pine Ridge and Rosebud reservations was moved farther east to the mouth of Black Pipe Creek, thus placing Lip's camp on the Pine Ridge Reservation, where his people continued to live among the Oglalas, insisting that they be counted on the Pine Ridge rolls (Feraca 1966:12; Pine Ridge Research Bulletin 1968:32; Utley 1963:78–79, 272–73).

Horn Chips settled here in the presence of Eagle Nest Butte. He continued to make pilgrimages to the top of the butte, fasting and praying for his people, until he died in 1916. But before dying he had managed to pass on his knowledge not only through his own family, but through other sacred persons like Black Horse who had served as apprentices to him. Here he performed marvelous feats that are still the subject of conversation among contemporary Yuwipi men. Standing Bear, the Oglala writer, identifies Chips, Last Horse, White Crow, and Sorrel Horse as among the miraculous thunder or stone dreamers who could make storms start and end at will:

Chips was another Stone Dreamer and his fame was wide among his people, for he would go into the sweat-bath and there locate lost articles or horses and absent people. While taking the purification ceremony the *tunkes* [*sic; tunkan*], or hot stones, brought great inspiration to Chips, so when he went to the place of vigil they came to him in spirit and offered him service. So Chips always carried stones, some of them painted in colors, in his medicine bag. When he was making medicine they would fly to him and they could be heard striking the tipi and after we moved into houses I have heard them dropping down the chimney

and have seen them lying about on the floor where they had fallen.
[Standing Bear 1933:208]

More characteristics of Horn Chips's rituals are noted by
Feraca:

> Certain elements among the Teton have often tried to expose the
> *yuwipi* men as frauds, usually without success. Horn Chips, now dead,
> can be considered one of those *yuwipi* men who has greatly added to the
> cult's popularity. For one thing his spirits spoke in many voices, and all
> his prophecies are said to have been fulfilled. Some years ago, by order
> of the Agency Superintendent, who was in charge of Pine Ridge
> Reservation, Horn Chip's [*sic*] meeting was held in a lighted room.
> Indian police were present and the police chief himself carefully tied
> and wrapped the *yuwipi* man. Lights flashed on the ceiling. Horn Chips
> was untied when the flashing ceased. It is understandable that many
> Teton refer to him as the "real *yuwipi* man." [Feraca 1963:36]

Feraca further clarifies the relationship between the spirits of
heyoka and the "little people" who are often present during contemporary Yuwipis:

> It is dubious that any *Yuwipi* man exclusively deals with "little people"
> today. Horn Chips probably did and George Poor Thunder may have
> featured them, but the majority of tied shamans are released by all sorts
> of creatures, including toads. [Feraca 1963:39]

Ruby, a physician at Pine Ridge, tells us about Horn Chips's first
vision, which he probably heard about from George Plenty Wolf in
the early 1950s:

> Horn Chip's [*sic*] family died when he was young. He went to live with
> his grandmother. The other children made so much fun of him that he
> decided to commit suicide. On his way to a lonely spot to end his life, he
> heard a voice who said it was that of the Great Spirit. The voice told
> Horn Chips not to kill himself, that he was destined to become a great
> man. Horn Chips was told to go to a high mountain, dig a hole four feet
> deep, cover it with boughs, and stay there four days with no food or
> drink. Horn Chips followed directions. When he was in the pit, he had
> a vision. A snake came to him from the Great Spirit and gave him his
> instructions. [Ruby 1955:52]

In the description above, the arrangement of the vision pit is
identical with that of Black Horse's, and it is clear that the high
mountain is Eagle Nest Butte, where eagles once were trapped in
pits of the sort Horn Chips was told to dig. The form of the contem-

porary vision quest, in which the candidates lie in a pit, may be a variant of the Chips vision; few authors before Ruby make any reference to this particular form of the vision quest.

In an interview with Eugene Fugle, the yuwipi man George Flesh discusses a number of important Yuwipi men, naming George Plenty Wolf, Willie Wound, Mark Big Road, Sam Moose (*sic;* Moves) Camp, Joe Ashley, Frank Fools Crow, and John Iron Rope, and he states "I have heard that Horn Chips was the first *Yuwipi* doctor" (Fugle 1966:20–21).

Up to this point all the authors I have cited are referring to the same Horn Chips of Lip's band. More recent references to "Chips," however, must be approached with some caution, because the connection between Horn Chips and contemporary Yuwipi is not only ideological, but genealogical. In an interview with the Chips (also Chipps) family of Wanblee in July 1977, it was pointed out that old man Chips had four "sons": Ellis, Joe, Joe Ashley, and Sam Moves Camp, the last two being the same mentioned by Flesh (above). Although they are called "sons" in English, I interpret the native kinship classification to mean that Ellis and Joe were brothers in the American usage, while Joe Ashley was a cousin and Moves Camp was a half-brother. Nevertheless, all of the second generation of the Chips family were practicing Yuwipi men at one time or another. Ellis has three sons, Charles, Phillip, and Godfrey; Godfrey Chips has been a Yuwipi man since age thirteen and is regarded as one of the most powerful of all contemporary Yuwipi men. But when the Oglalas refer to the original Chips, they mean the medicine man who died in 1916.

In addition to the lack of clarity about the origin of yuwipi, there is disagreement over how Yuwipi may be classified in a broader context. For example, Feraca has pointed out that the Oglala do not regard Yuwipi as a membership church (in the manner of the Native American Church or Christian sects), stating:

Membership in Yuwipi, if we may use the term, is determined solely by attendance at "meetings" (the Sioux rarely use the word "ceremony"). Any full blood, or a borderline mixed blood, who attends at least one meeting or "sing" *(lowanpi)* during the year, can be classed as a Yuwipi devotee. Initiations are unknown, except in the case of one shaman confiding in another or instructing a neophyte. The devotees are participants insofar as the adult male usually partake of the sweat bath preceding the ceremony, and all "help the Yuwipi man sing," while the meeting is in progress. [1963:26]

Feraca views Yuwipi as a "cult," as do Hurt and Howard (1952:286), Macgregor 1946:98), and Fugle (1966:1). Fugle misunderstands native categories when he classifies cult meetings in three distinct groups—Yuwipi, night cults, and eagle medicine cult (and similar cults)—using as a common denominator for all Lakota rituals held at night the term *hanhepi*, literally "night," stating:

> I believe that it is rather naive to classify certain other similar cults under the general term, *Yuwipi*. It should be understood that the term, *Yuwipi*, refers only to a specific cult. Although *some* Oglala generally refer to any cult meeting taking place in darkness as *Yuwipi*, a more accurate classification which *many* of the Oglala devotees themselves use is simply *Hanhepi*, or Nighttime [italics added]

Fugle thinks it naive to classify similar cults under the general term Yuwipi, but he does not make a distinction between what *some* Oglalas do and what *many* others do. His "more accurate" classification, *hanhepi*, simply does not hold with Oglala perceptions of night cult meetings. *Hanhepi* means night, but it cannot be used specifically or generally to mean "meeting" or "sings." Under *hanhepi* he discusses Yuwipi (proper), eagle medicine cult (and similar cults that invoke the power of birds and animals), and *hanhepi woecun*, literally "night doings." Fugle recognized that no matter what the variation of the meeting is, all are related to the older "dream cults" described by Wissler (1912) and Lowie (1913); however, there has never been a Lakota common denominator for all these variations other than *ihanblapi* (they dream of), and this term always specifically referred to a congregation of people sharing similar dreams—for example, *mato ihanblapi* 'they dream of bears.'

Malan and Jesser conclude that Yuwipi is marginal to older forms of Oglala traditional religion (1959:48–49), and I would join Feraca in disagreeing with this position. Yuwipi, however classified, embodies all the ideological elements inherent in traditional Oglala precepts. Only negligible influences of Christianity are found (but cf. Steinmetz 1980 for an opposing point of view), and certainly not to the degree that they are found in the Native American Church.

Feraca is correct in stating that the Oglalas refer to Yuwipi as a meeting when speaking English and as a "sing" (*lowanpi*) when speaking Lakota. However, his criteria for classifying someone as a Yuwipi "devotee" are rather arbitrary. The Oglalas do not insist that the follower of Yuwipi ideology be a full blood or a "borderline mixed blood" (whatever that means), nor is it necessary for someone to attend "at least one meeting during the year." If, by attending the meeting, the "devotees" participate, then they may be called participants, but some persons may not attend Yuwipi meetings for years. All who wish to may join in the singing, but they do so to help out the recognized singer or singers, as well as the Yuwipi man.

If it is necessary to classify curative meetings, or meetings held in darkness to solicit supernatural aid, it is better to discuss the subject from the Oglala point of view. But first it must be made clear that the Oglalas perceive Yuwipi or any variant as only part of a greater ideology that transcends any single ritual variant. The traditional ideology that is constantly evolving may be intensified by ritual performance, but ritual performance is only one aspect of traditional belief. Yuwipi, then, represents only a ritual microcosm in the Oglalas' cultural macrocosmic world view. Whether one kind of spirit (a bear or an eagle) or another is invoked does establish a system of variant rituals, but it does not alter the total corpus of ideological concepts.

Contemporary Oglalas, especially the older generation, strongly relate what is "Indian" to what is *wakan,* the latter term being the Lakota equivalent of the mana concept. This is to say, there is a strong feeling among older Oglalas that the Indian ways are disappearing; as traditional beliefs and customs wane, there is a need to associate *wakan* concepts with them even if they were originally secular in nature. The further the contemporary Oglalas are divorced in time from traditional beliefs, the stronger the attempt to identify these beliefs as religious rather than secular. In short, many secular ceremonies, dances, songs, and artifacts are invested with a *wakan* attribute, even though they were not so regarded in olden times. Many older Oglalas speak of things as being *Lakol wicoȟ'an* Indian way (literally Indian acts, actions, or even mannerisms). Yuwipi and other religious institutions are "classified" under *Lakol wicoȟ'an,* as are secular institutions such as the grass dance, rabbit dance, and war stories (because the heroes of these stories lived in a time when Indian "power" was strong and thus were capable of performing deeds that are no longer possible). To the Oglalas, "the Indian way" connotes a holistic concept that vividly conjures up the religious and secular mannerisms of the old-time Indian.

In modern times, when the influence of the white man prevails, rituals become an intense focal point of the Indian Way, a time to recapture the old times, the "sacred" times when the power of the Indian was strong and in no way diminished by white contact. The rituals provide the right milieu for the Indians gathered to act *tokel ikce wicaša hecel ecunpi,* in the manner of the old-timers. Thus in the

Yuwipi ritual an ordinary frame house is transformed into the *hocoka,* the camp circle, and all generations of Indians as well as all constituents of the Oglala universe are brought together to solidify what is conceived as Indian.

The prerequisite for attending or participating in Yuwipi (or vision quest, or sweat lodge) is simply belief in the Indian Way. One must believe, because if he does not the rituals will not be effective; the spirits will refuse to enter a dwelling where skeptics are present. Stories regarding the discontinuation of meetings because fantastic things happened to disbelievers are abundant on the reservation. The need to believe is not imposed on the individual by the Yuwipi man or by any dogma. The individual decides for himself whether he accepts the precepts of religious ideology.

If an Oglala believes in the Indian Way, he becomes aware that he has an obligation that is an integral part of sustaining Indian culture. He will be criticized or acknowledged by members of his society according to his willingness and ability to "help out." It must be stressed that the Oglala concept of "helping out," expressed in the verb *okiya* 'to help' or the noun *wookiye* 'help', is critical to understanding the full meaning of the Indian Way.

In the Lakota language, virtually every form of participation, attendance, or actual assistance in religious and secular events is expressed by the concept "to help out." To the Oglalas, helping out signifies not only actively assisting someone in a task, but also passively supporting the task. The Oglalas measure the success of any communal undertaking by the number of people in attendance. Perhaps this is true of all societies; but the Oglalas, feeling that the Indian Way is dying out, place more importance on attendance because the more people there are at a function, especially an Indian function, the less chance there is that the function will disappear. Thus mere attendance is deemed a "helping out" of a function, whether it is religious or secular. In the snake dance, a popular powwow dance of the 1960s, the dancers follow the leader in a serpentine pattern through the dance arbor for the sole purpose of letting the powwow committee count the number of dancers (Powers 1968). The total count of any dance is the subject of conversation long after the dance has ended. Inquiring about the success of a dance, the Oglalas will always ask how many dancers and drums (groups of singers) were there.

Thus the dancers dress up and go to the dance because they like to dance, but they are also aware that they are helping out the people by doing so. Powwows are often difficult to get started, and the first man in costume may be awarded a cash prize because the Oglalas know that once the first man is "on the floor" others will follow.

When a person known as a singer passes a group of men at the drum he will be asked not to "join them" or to "sing with them," but rather to "help them out," the act of singing being implied. The good singer is one who helps out, that is, sings all portions of the songs all the time so that no single singer must carry the song by himself.

During the giveaways at powwows, money is given to dancers, attendants, and singers in a formal way through the intercession of an *eyapaha* 'announcer.' The formula is always "The mother [or whomever] of so and so would like *help out* the singers (or whomever) by giving them two dollars." One never simply *gives* them money. In Lakota, the concept of giving to help out often takes the form of a compound verb "to help out by giving" (*k'u okiya*), as in *nicupi oniciyapelo* 'she gives you; she helps you out.'

Often the concept of helping out becomes hierarchical. The Oglala is first obliged to help out those he calls *mitakuyepi* 'my relations,' then the general *tiyošpaye* 'band' or *oti* 'community', then *oyate* 'the people.'

White Calf, a close friend for twenty years, was once planning to sing for a dance he knew I was going to attend. Early in the evening before the dance started, he sent his son to my house with a note:

> How Kola: I am sorry I can't be with you tonight but my people are having a dance at Slim Buttes and I have to help them out.

By Oglala standards this was a sufficient "excuse," and no apology was really necessary.

At community meetings, memorial feasts, and wakes, everyone living in the community, or related to the family sponsoring the event, is expected to help out with food, money, and attendance. Even a person who has not donated any material goods will often be acknowledged by someone's saying, "He traveled a long way to help us out." Oglalas who have stayed with me at my home off the reservations have always offered thanks for my hospitality in specific terms. I have "helped them out with a place to stay, with food to eat," and with other amenities normally provided to any house guest.

Just as people are regarded for the way they help out others, they acknowledge subjectively that others "depend on them." An Oglala is obliged to do things because "they depend on me." Thus a singer must go to a dance because "the people depend on me." He must share his wages with nonworking members of his family because they depend on his support. The binding factor here is that "it is the

Indian Way." Some young people working in Community Action
Programs feel impelled to spend whatever money they earn immediately, because they know that under the Indian Way they will be
obliged to share their income with whatever members of the family
are destitute. It is precisely this dichotomy between the Indian values
of cooperation and the non-Indian's concept of competition that
creates anxiety in the traditional Oglala community.

Yuwipi is only a microcosm of the Indian Way, and it is not
surprising that the concept of sustaining and solidifying Indian
"things," of helping out, is a predominant part of the congregational
aspect of the meeting. Participating actively, then, is not a
prerequisite for attendance. Just being at the meeting is helping out
by Oglala standards. It remains to be seen whether the Oglalas really
conceive of "attendance" or "participation" in meetings, or whether
we can accurately call those who help out at Yuwipi meetings "devotees," or whether any other term of classification can be applied,
no matter how convenient. It is also interesting to analyze just how
"some" or "many" Oglalas classify religious meetings.

As I stated earlier, the Oglalas call the night rituals "meetings" in
English and *lowanpi* 'sings' in Lakota. While they recognize that each
shaman conducts his own meetings in a special way, different from
that of other shamans, there is still a tendency to call all meetings
Yuwipi meetings. The phenomenon is simply referred to as Yuwipi.
One shaman may conduct "a different kind of Yuwipi," but what was
once a term for meetings in which the shaman was wrapped and tied
has become a generic term for all night meetings.

In addition, the term Yuwipi is used in other ways by the Oglalas
when they speak English. Not only do people help out at a Yuwipi
meeting, they are Yuwipi. Expression like "those Yuwipis always
come to the meeting" or "I'm afraid of those Yuwipis" (in both cases
referring to the spirits) are common. Songs sung during the ritual
are known as Yuwipi songs. Oglalas may say of a person who goes
regularly to meetings, "He's Yuwipi." But a Yuwipi man can only
mean the shaman who conducts the meeting.

The term Yuwipi apparently is being used more generically today
than when Yuwipi was related specifically to tying rites. But as the
variants, eagle doctoring, bear doctoring, and the like, began to
diminish, Yuwipi became popular as a classification, at least in English. I have heard one young Sicangu say in frustration at trying to
convince a white man that he followed the Indian Way, *yuwipi hemaca*
'I am Yuwipi.' And in 1970 the Indian motion picture star Iron Eyes

Cody, a Cherokee, signed an autograph at the Pine Ridge sun dance for an Oglala man by writing "Your Yuwipi friend."

While some practitioners of Yuwipi may in fact say that their particular meetings are not Yuwipi, but rather eagle doctoring or whatever, the term Yuwipi is understood by everyone in the Indian community, whereas variations may not be.

There continues to be a growing interest in Yuwipi and Yuwipi-like rituals both at Pine Ridge and at other Sioux reservations, and Yuwipi men from Pine Ridge, Rosebud, and Cheyenne River have introduced the ritual to other tribes as well. There is also increased scholarly interest in Yuwipi. Recently, for example, we have seen a rash of publications on Lakota religion, some of which include biographical sketches of medicine men (Buechel 1978; Fire and Erdoes 1972; Mails 1979); on mythology (Theisz 1975); and on ritual (Erdoes 1972; Mails 1978); as well as general works, both new and reprinted (Powers 1977; Walker 1980).

Whatever its origins, Yuwipi continues to develop as a ritual whose symbols represent all that is significant to the Indian Way. It is quite possible that it may become the most meaningful expression of Oglala spiritual values in the years to come.

Prelude

If you stare at the expanses of land surrounding Pine Ridge, you are overwhelmed by vast space, by miles of rolling hills and chalky buttes where cone-shaped pines stand sentrylike above the reservation. The longer you gaze the more you feel you are looking at a painted landscape; everything seems two-dimensional, a canvas of multicolored meadows and bluffs. The purples and lavenders of aromatic asters mingle with those of wild prairie turnips; ice meadow rose and fireweed challenge the showy hoary aster; yellow leafy spurge and tumble mustard are dwarfed by sunflowers and black-eyed Susans; pale evening primrose and grassy death camas are swept by brooms of white prairie clover. Time and space seem to mesh, creating a mural like the early paintings of Oscar Howe and Andrew Standing Soldier, famous Lakota artists who really saw the land.

This illusion springs partly from the form of the land itself— predominantly rolling hills. Intricate networks of roads, particularly ancient wagon roads, shoot over the hills and disappear before their symmetrical ruts carved into the soft gumbo by a hundred years of wheels, converge to a point; you are cut off from any sense of perspective. This disjunction between visual reality and cognitive reality, with the first gaining primacy, makes the painting of the Lakota artists seem realistic rather than stylized, though they never paint in a style that Euro-Americans would regard as three-dimensional.

Once your view of the terrain has adjusted to the contradiction, it is shattered by occasional movement. On peacefully overcast days, Pine Ridge seems static; there is little motion. But on sunny days, or when there are fast-moving clouds—the kind Oglalas call the Grandfathers—ancient spirits rolling over the land on their way home—on such days the image is less like a painting than like a motion picture. The two-dimensionality remains, but there are changes in the scene: a flash of sunlight; fine-edged shadows where clouds pass between the sun and the earth; stabbing flickers where cylinders of lightning strike. Now the scene becomes less like a motion picture than a montage of still photos, disrupting one's sense of continuous movement.

On calm days any movement becomes an event: a devil duster ricocheting off cutbanks like a stone skipped across a pond; the flash of a flicker racing up a telephone pole. Here, where sight reaches farther than sound, a small herd of horses breaks the skyline, stands motionless, then darts off. And at dawn the sun bobs over the backs of white-faced cattle as if it were, as the Lakotas say, an old man dancing.

During our noon meal Zona turned her attention first to a figure coming over the rise east of the house, then to another approaching from town. We all stopped eating and watched. The two moved slowly toward each other, a story unfolding before us. The figures traveling the blacktop road would have to meet. The road ran east and west from Pine Ridge Village to Slim Buttes before veering off into the white man's land. It was noon, and the temperature was at ninety degrees, where it had remained for nearly a week. Perhaps fifteen minutes passed before there was silent agreement on the identity of the two figures: from the west came Loves War, after his morning visit with his old friends at the chief's house; from the east came Plenty Wolf, carrying a bag of groceries. Though the old men knew each other, Plenty Wolf was nearly blind from glaucoma and thus unaware that this friend was half a mile from him. Loves War knew this; he knew all the people at Red Cloud Community, though he now lived at Oglala, eighteen miles away. He had been staying in the community with relatives to await the coming

Sun dance celebration. He, like everyone else, knew that Plenty Wolf was old, at the end of his career—that like all sacred persons in every community on the reservation he was losing his power. Soon he would no longer receive visions. Soon he could no longer counsel people with the pipe, and, most important, no longer cure them in the spirit meetings. Plenty Wolf was going blind, and his ability as a sacred person would diminish and die. He would become a common man, taunted and ridiculed by some who had called him Grand-father and besought him to intercede for them with the Grand-fathers and the animal guardians living between earth and sky.

As the two men walked steadily toward each other, we returned to eating but kept our eyes on them. Although we could not hear, we knew their first words would be about the heat wave. That these two should be out on the road at high noon was not really surprising. The old people complain about the heat and cold not so much because they are senile or suffer from poor circulation as because they place themselves in situations that the young avoid. In their prime these men would have traveled at dawn, or perhaps in the evening. But this day they trudged through the heat complaining, *"Lila kate. Lila temni mat'e."* "It's really hot. The heat is killing me."

The two men in the middle of the road, Plenty Wolf at first straining to recognize Loves War. They shook hands, exchanged a few words, and passed on, each continuing his own way. Zona gave a sigh of relief, and everyone laughed as if it were the punch line of a long-drawn-out joke. Each man turned off on a different gumbo road, Loves War seeking out more old friends and Plenty Wolf going home to his log cabin and the deliberations of his sacred pipe.

The roads that transect the Pine Ridge Reservation symbolize the places where they lead. The modern blacktops lead to bureau-cracy and ultimately to Washington, D.C. Over these roads you pass through a hundred years of federal civilization programs, through towns where there lie buried the roots of the original seven Oglala bands, or *tiyošpayes*, as they are called in Lakota: Pushed Aside, Spleen, Cut-offs, Wajajes, Bad Faces, Untidy, and Loafers. These bands settled along the creeks, and eventually their settlements became communities with less colorful appellations: Manderson, Kyle, Oglala, Hisle, Allen, Wounded Knee, Porcupine, Slim Buttes, Batesland, and Pine Ridge Village, the last being the original Indian agency and still the seat of political authority. Tipis and travois gave way to log cabins and box wagons, and new housing developments rose like mirages on the rolling prairies. One may follow the blacktops through progress, technological achievement, and Christianity.

Gravel roads lead to community garbage dumps and cemeteries. The dumps lie in bulldozed hollows: abandoned cars, discarded clothing, food, and dead animals contribute to a stench that announces the presence of a dump for miles around. Only magpies haunt the refuse, pecking at rotting carrion and bouncing from fencepost to fencepost, tempting the religious to pluck their tail feathers to make a sacred fan.

The graves are on hills, marked with weathered crosses and plastic flowers left from Memorial Day or the Fourth of July. Fresh paint does little to hide the vulnerability of the grave posts, and surely it must be the benevolence of the Great Spirit that prevents the dust of the graves from scattering over Mother Earth.

Then there are the old wagon roads, cut into the gumbo that geologists call the Pierre Formation. Gumbo is a soil characteristic of South Dakota; it is sandy and abrasive when dry, but buttery when wet. After a heavy rain it is almost impossible to drive over these roads, and until the ground dries each car simply recuts the grooves. Because of constant regrooving, these wagon roads are indelibly etched into the land, though today many of them lead only to deserted homesteads where the old people lived before federal programs coaxed them into "new housing" (pronounced locally as if it were one word).

Although one can cross the reservation on these roads, they are used less and less. In some cases the wagon roads are graveled over and later blacktopped. Most are left as local historical markers—it may be said that a famous chief used to live down this road, or that if you follow that road you will come to the place where a cowboy is buried. Yet sometimes at the end of the road you find a log house or two occupied by traditional Oglalas who have managed to resist the luxuries along the blacktops. Ideally these homesteads are near a creek, where there is plenty of water and firewood. The oldest were built in the early 1870s, and they stand as witnesses to the Oglalas' drastic change of life-style.

Some of the roads are more daring: they lead to canyons and buttes, though they stop abruptly before the ascent or descent. If one is to venture farther one must go on horseback or on foot, not because wagons and automobiles cannot make the grade, but because these are considered sacred places, and the white man's technology is not permitted. From a distance the hills are misleading. They resemble wavy lines silhouetted against the horizon like a child's picture of the ocean. But in approaching them on foot you become aware of their formidable height. As you draw near, the ground slopes downhill, yet you are unaware of it until the hills seem about to topple over you. The grade changes abruptly to uphill, and you realize the ordeal you must face to reach the summit. As you climb, your footsteps become measured; you dig your toes into crevices and grab onto withering sagebrush to keep from sliding down the slippery prairie grass. When you reach the top you are struck by the wholeness of nature: you can see far in every direction, and you realize how much more you know about the world than the people down below. Then you are overcome by the price you pay for this knowledge: you are alone.

There are places on the Pine Ridge Reservation where no roads go. They are not particularly sacred; there are no spirits there, at least not in the daytime. It is best to go there in spring, when wildflowers are blooming and the earth has not yet turned brown and dusty. The most abundant tree is the western yellow pine, interspersed with red cedar and juniper. Cottonwoods and willows cluster along the creek banks. The Oglalas considered them sacred because they can be rooted from slips, and they are regarded as living beings, symbolic of life itself. The cottonwood serves as the sacred pole during the Sun dance, and the willow provides saplings for the sweat lodge.

In the wooded ravines that relieve the boredom of the rolling hills grow numbers of edible plants: currants, wild rose, red plum, buffalo berry, coral berry, and the pervasive chokecherry. The last which ripens in late July and August, entices people to these special places, where they eat great amounts of berries right off the bushes, emerging with black teeth and parched throats. On smooth, grassy places, lavender flowers are guides to *tinpsila*, the sweet prairie turnips whose succulent roots lie beneath the earth.

These *pommes blanches*, as the French call them, were once a staple for the Oglalas. In the spring families still gather the turnips with digging sticks and crowbars. They can be eaten raw by slipping off the outer skin, for they are sweet and juicy, more like carrots than like our domesticated turnips. For the most part the people gather them for soups and stews. They are peeled for drying, and the stems are woven together to form a long chain of hard white bulbs that are later reconstituted by soaking.

The characteristic form from which the reservation derives its name is the chalky white buttes that rise above the rolling hills. The buttes are speckled with scraggly yellow pines, some straight, others growing out of the sides of the buttes and contorted by the constant prairie winds. The southern boundary of the reservation lies along the Nebraska state line. From the Platte River north to Pine Ridge one finds the thinly grassed "dead dunes" called the sand hills. These sand hills cover roughly 18,000 square miles and, like most of the High Plains, offer little timber, water, or arable land. Here a variety of cacti, soapweed, and yucca hide between patches of sagebrush and the skeletal remains of tumbleweeds that bounce across the dunes like coral floating on the currents of some vast ocean.

The parched gray green of the sand hills receives an occasional dousing, and for a few hours the land is revitalized and emits odors of sage and sweet grass. Clear skies suddenly give way to great cumulus clouds, like free-form sculpture, that slowly begin to move, then gradually increase their velocity. The skies turn gray, and clouds fishtail and roll so close to the earth that you believe you could touch them with your fingers. Lightning stabs the earth in vertical bars and magnetic curtains. Clouds explode through the sky, and the earth seems about to crack like glass. The parched ground is covered with streams rushing in every direction. Creeks that lay sluggish in their beds are awakened to rush headlong among trees, roads, and dunes. Gumbo and gravel melt into pools, and flash floods stack mud deposits.

Then the Thunder-Beings' voices diminish to a murmur. Their eyes close, sucking up what is left of the lightning. Hooded giants on particolored horses drive their slaves homeward to the hills in the west, firmly holding their leashes of lightning. The gods have made their presence known so the people may understand that human arrogance is not permitted—that men are antlike figures humbly crawling across the universe, no more and no less important than the other creatures of the world.

Pine Ridge has settled down. The vapor trail of a jet bound for Rapid City streaks the sky. Children look up at the rainbow, and their grandparents warn them not to point at it lest their fingers swell. For here at the end of gumbo roads nature still controls human destiny, and it teaches that people should be mindful of their relatives and remember their responsibilities to other Oglalas. Here sacred pipes wait to be unwrapped and smoked, and bonds between nature and culture are firmly established. Here even the white man's technology is subservient to cosmos and kin.

Sacred Stones

Every Oglala who believes in the omnipotence of Wakantanka wears or carries a small spherical stone carefully rolled up in a wad of sage and deposited neatly in a miniature buckskin pouch no more than an inch in diameter. Men normally wear these pouches pinned inside their shirts, and women carry them in their purses. It is not necessary to carry these stones on one's person every day, but if one is about to embark upon some important mission, such as a trip off the reservation, or if one wishes to invoke the aid of the supernaturals, one carries the stone with him.

Inhering in each stone is a spirit called *šicun*, understood as that aspect of the soul that lasts forever and is capable of being reinvested in another object, human or nonhuman, animate or inanimate, at one's death. Not all *šicuns* are reinvested, so there is always a surplus, some of which may be called upon in a ritual to perform certain acts dealing mainly with curing or to reveal information necessary for the welfare of the people.

Each of the *šicuns*, or spirits as they are called locally in English, has a name. These stone spirits reveal themselves to sacred persons and are employed by the Yuwipi men to help them cure the sick and find lost or stolen objects. When individually owned, that is, inhering in the personal stone of an individual, the spirits protect that person from danger, hunger, financial problems, and marital difficulties—in short, any of the crises an Oglala is likely to encounter, or may fear encountering, during his or her lifetime. An individual's personal stone possesses a tutelary spirit, analogous to the Christian guardian angel, but with one important difference. Whereas in Christianity one guardian spirit may be signed to an indefinite number of people, each Oglala has an exclusive protecting spirit. During a crisis, an Oglala may pray directly to the spirit for aid or counsel. As long as he does not offend the spirit, he is guaranteed of its protection throughout his life. When he dies, the spirit leaves his stone and is free to inhere in another's stone.

Anyone who so desires may acquire such a stone through a special ritual called *Inktomi lowanpi* 'Spider sing.' The name of this ritual underscored the important relationship between the stone spirits and Inktomi, the cosmological character who predates the emergence of humans from a subterranean existence to life on the earth and was responsible for teaching the original Lakota how to live as cultural beings. Explicit in Inktomi's personality and deeds is his dualistic nature. He is capable of transforming himself into any object, but his natural appearance is that of a spider. He is at once the personification of good and evil, pride and humility, knowledge and ignorance, maleness and femaleness, child and adult, and stories that reflect this duality are told, particularly to children, to teach them proper social conduct in Oglala society. The lessons are all negative, because Inktomi's adventures exemplify improper conduct. If one learns *not* to do what Inktomi does in his cyclical adventures, one will grow up to be a respectable and responsible member of the community.

Inktomi himself has an interesting genealogy that again emphasizes the relationship between the stone spirits and Spider. Inktomi is the progeny of a union between Inyan the Rock, the oldest form of creation, and Wakinyan, the Thunder-Beings who manifest themselves in thunder and lightning and are invoked by common people to cleanse the earth of filth and evil. Inktomi has one brother, Iya the Glutton, who is generally depicted as an icy giant with a large head and rather small body. He goes about the world trying to satisfy his insatiable hunger by devouring humans. When the two brothers meet there is constant argument over which has primacy based on birth order. There is little to be learned from Iya's androphagous meanderings except perhaps that an individual's gluttony can lead to the destruction of others. But Inktomi has learned to deal with his brother's wicked behavior. He follows him around and instructs people to light a fire under him if he has consumed their loved ones. The fire causes Iya to melt and regurgitate his human meal. Thus, despite Inktomi's own mischievous deeds and the pranks he plays on humanity, he ultimately benefits people by saving them from a cannibalistic death.

Some of the stone spirits are named after Inktomi's attributes—Flying Spider, Spider Who Walks Underground, Spider Who Walks on the Water, Spider Who Respects Nothing, Spider Who Destroys Things, Spider Who Argues with Everyone. During the special Inktomi sing, the specific *šicun* that is to become a tutelary spirit is invested in an otherwise common stone, and during the ritual act it is said that the "stone is named." Thus the naming (*caštun*) itself renders the profane stone sacred and potent.

Any adept who wishes to obtain a spirit may request the appropriate ritual and may go out and search for his own stone, which he later brings to the Yuwipi man. He may also have a buckskin pouch made for the occasion, and during the naming ritual the spirits will place the stone in the pouch in the darkness; it will be returned to the owner at the conclusion of the ritual. Often, however, a person asks the Yuwipi man to provide both the stone (in some cases more than one) and the buckskin pouch.

If the person brings his own stone, it must be perfectly spherical and is usually found in the bed of a creek, river, or lake. A Yuwipi man will usually try to find such a stone near an anthill, where these industrious creatures have pushed it up to the surface. The Oglalas believe that the surface of the earth is contaminated, but that the earth beneath is clean. Thus the natural objects one finds around any burrow are particularly efficacious for religious purposes. Animals and insects that go back and forth between the surface of the earth and the underground have knowledge of both worlds and themselves form a fraternity whose members may be called upon to aid the people. Thus spiders, ants, moles, prairie dogs, wolves, coyotes, and snakes, though different in anatomy and behavior, are linked in the religious precepts because of their two-worldliness, and the earth and stones found around their homes are particularly efficacious for promoting personal security and welfare.

An ordinary stone of any kind is called *inyan*, and a pile of rocks is called *ih'e*. But these special spherical stones in which one's tutelary spirit resides are called *tunkan* and are related to the kinship term *tunkasila* 'grandfather.' When the spirit is invested in the stone and the stone is placed in the pouch, the amulet is called *tunkan wašicun*, roughly 'spirit of the stone.' The stone, like all *šicun* in the universe, may be addressed honorifically as *Tunkašila* during prayers and songs, and the term may also refer to the collective *šicun*: animals, stones, birds, and other animate and inanimate objects. In some cases it may be used to address a specific *šicun*.

There are a finite number of *šicun* in the universe, and these types are very loosely related to the Western notion of species. The people say that everything that walks on two legs, on four legs, everything that crawls or flies, everything that swims or burrows, everything that grows out of the earth, everything that resides in the heavens has a *šicun*. Together there are 405 types or species. When an Oglala wants to call upon all the types of *šicun* in the universe he must prepare one tobacco offering for each of them. Each tobacco offering, called *canli wapaňte* 'tobacco bundle,' is made from a one-inch square of cotton cloth into which a minute pinch of tobacco has been placed; the cloth is shaped into a small ball and tied with a string. During certain rituals such as the vision quest and Yuwipi, all 405 tobacco offerings are tied to one string that is used to delineate a sacred area metaphorically called the *hocoka*. *Hocoka* is an old word that refers to the inner part of a camp circle, but as used ritually it means a sacred space, the center of the universe, within which a sacred person or supplicant prays, sings, or otherwise communicates with spirits. During the ritual the spirits who attend pick up the essence of the tobacco the people have offered in thanksgiving and take it back to their homes, where it is shared with the *šicun* of the universe and smoked.

There are two other kinds of tobacco offerings, fashioned in the same way but used somewhat differently. The first is sometimes called the "short string" because it contains a small number of tobacco offerings. These offerings are intended for a selected number of spirits who are the most powerful assistants of the sacred person. The second kind contains only seven offerings, made exclusive of any ritual by people who want to offer up personal prayers. The most effective way of doing this is to walk into the hills and hang the tobacco offerings in a tree and pray to the Four Winds, the Sky, the Earth, and the Spotted Eagle who carries prayers upward to Wakantanka. Often people who cannot participate in a sweat lodge for one reason or another ask the Yuwipi man to take their personal offerings into the lodge and hang them from the willow framework, where they will be taken up by some of the spirits who attend the ritual.

The sacred stones and other *šicuns*, when invoked to aid the sacred persons during the vision quest, sweat lodge, and Yuwipi rituals, also respond favorably to colored cloth flags called *wanunyanpi* 'offerings' when they are raised around the sacred places. The cloth flags usually are made of half a yard of cotton material, and each color symbolizes a direction: the west, black; the north, red; the east, yellow; the south, white. Raising these flags at one of the rituals will cause the sacred stones living at the four quarters of the universe to fly to the meeting place. Most frequently, only four of these flags are raised for the vision quest. Each is placed carefully at one of the four cardinal points of the sacred place, and they are connected by the long string of tobacco offerings. At Yuwipis, however, two more flags are added: blue for the sky and Takuškanškan, the power that gives movement to all things; and green for the earth, Maka Ina, Mother Earth, from whose bosom all things grow and nourish themselves. Some sacred persons use a seventh offering that may be composed of cloth offerings or of various natural objects such as animal hair and fur, feathers, shells, bone, and bits of wood—all things of a very personal nature that are symbolic of their own power—that they have been instructed to use in their own vision quests.

Finally, there is one other kind of sacred stone that Oglalas recognize as the most powerful of all. Called *iyanša* 'red stone' in Lakota and catlinite in English, it is quarried near Pipestone, Minnesota. This stone is highly valued by many plains tribes, and according to the Oglala sacred persons it is red because it is made partly from the blood of an older people, antecedents of the Lakota, who died in a great primordial flood.

The sacred red stone is used primarily to make sacred pipes that are filled and smoked whenever it is necessary to communicate with Wakantanka, the Tunkašilas, the *šicuns,* or any of the spirits of humans, animals, birds, and stones—all animate and inanimate objects capable of helping living people.

As is well known, the pipe was brought to the Lakota people by White Buffalo Calf Woman, with instructions on how to use it when praying and singing to Wakantanka. It is the most significant instrument of prayer in all of the rituals, and without it it is impossible to make contact with the benevolent spirits that live beneath the earth, on the surface of the earth, or between the earth and the sky.

When someone is troubled, or ill, or has problems with his family, when someone is in need of money or has difficulty with the tribal office or with white men in town, or when someone is about to leave the reservation to visit friends or relatives in the cities, to go into the armed forces, or attend school in some faraway place, he should use the pipe. People may need help and assistance from the supernaturals to ensure that they can fulfill their needs, live happy lives, and combat the ever-present obstacles set before them by the white bureaucrats; the ranchers and farmers who lease their land; the teachers who try to shape their children's minds; those in office who control financial resources and grants for higher education; those in the Bureau of Indian Affairs in Washington or its local representative, the superintendent; those in the tribal council or law enforcement agencies; the tribal court; those missionaries who cajole the parents to send their children away to school where they will forever be lost to their people—for all these things, for all these problems, the solution lies in praying to Wakantanka with *cannunpa wakan,* the sacred pipe. For, as White Buffalo Calf Woman instructed, the pipe will protect the people from all harm, and those who want to live a long and healthy life with their relations—all their relations—should fill the pipe and smoke it, pointing its mouthpiece to the horizon, that place between the earth and the sky where the powerful spirits dwell, and pray first to the west, then to the north, then to the east, then to the south. They should then point the mouthpiece high into the sky and pray to the power that generates and moves everything; then to the earth; then to Wanbli Gleška, the Spotted Eagle who will carry the prayers, the intentions, the needs, and the wants of the people to Wakantanka.

They should cry out to Wakantanka in a loud voice:

Wakantanka unšimala ye. Mitakuye ob wani kta ca lecamun welo.
Wakantanka pity me. I want to live with all my relations; that is why I am doing this.

Any Oglala wishing to sponsor a Yuwipi may do so. He will first smoke alone, using a pipe or cigarette, and deliberate over his intentions for holding such a meeting. He will then seek out a Yuwipi man to serve as an intercessor and to conduct the appropriate ritual.

Such was the case with Runs Again, who in his seventieth year had been suffering from a pain in his back. It was not constant; some days he felt fine. But without warning the pain would return, and he would lie on his cot and stare at the wall waiting for his misery to pass.

Not many attended to the old man. All his children had married and moved away, some to Denver, some to Chicago. All, that is, but his son Wayne, who remained with Runs Again. But Wayne was not much consolation for the old man. Wayne stayed out late at nights and sometimes was gone for days at a time. He was finishing high school and had made ambitious plans to go to college with some of his friends. But things did not work out: he met a girl who became pregnant and gave birth to a baby boy. People gossiped that the baby looked just like him. But Wayne denied paternity and spent a good deal of time avoiding the people in the community, particularly the girl and her parents.

He tried unsuccessfully to leave Pine Ridge. He considered picking beets in Idaho or relocating in Denver or Chicago. Once he even planned to go to Los Angeles. But he had a hard time getting past Jumping Eagle's saloon in White Clay, or the H and N Café in Rushville, or any of the other bars where young men and women his age congregated. Day after day and night after night he sat in bars drinking "red beer" or swigged cheap wine on lovers' lane just across the reservation border. He became a target for the Pine Ridge police, who waited at the line to haul drunks away to the Pine Ridge jail. Morning after morning he woke up to the South Dakota heat and to armies of flies marching across his parched lips, then dashed to the water bucket to eliminate the choking aftermath of a wine drunk.

Now he agonized over the sight of his father staring at barren walls, shifting position on his cot to alleviate the pain. Wayne was despondent and bored, but he was helpless to aid the old man or to help himself.

Runs Again considered himself one of the last of his generation, as old men are apt to do. He had seen his wife, his kind, and his friends die off one by one, and he felt empty watching his final days pass without the good times and companionship he had known in his younger years. But most of all he felt hollow inside because he had taken his youth for granted. Now everything was gone—not only his kin and friends, but his ways, the traditional ways of his generation—skimmed away by a new generation of whites and a new generation of Indians. He had waited too long to enjoy his life as an Oglala. Now old age was overtaking him, and with it loneliness and isolation and a confounding pain that would not let him rest.

Wayne became more Indian when he drank. He would speak Lakota and talk about the old days that he knew only secondhand through his father and some of the older people. One day he awoke still half-drunk and found his father fondling an old buckskin bag that always hung on a nail in the wall. The old man was crying, and tears flowed heavily down his cheeks. The sight was too much for Wayne, and he too began to cry, first softly and then loudly. And as he wept he began to pray in Indian fashion, calling on Wakantanka to pity him and his father because they were both *unšike* 'pitiable,' and he cried out that he knew he was no good but that there was no reason his father should suffer for it. At first on impulse, then with resolve, he ran out of the house, clutching the old man's pouch, and jumped into his pickup truck. He raced the engine and took off in a hail of gravel down the road toward Slim Buttes. At the junction, he whipped around the corner so all that could be seen was the thick trail of dust that followed his tracks. He drove like a madman, perhaps still half-drunk, until he reached the house of Plenty Wolf.

The Sweat Lodge: Inside

There are many kinds of dreamers among the Oglalas: some have dreamed of the eagle, bear, elk, or other animals; some have dreamed of birds. The Yuwipi man is only one kind, and he receives his first instructions about the duties of the Yuwipi man in a vision that may be incomprehensible to him and require the interpretation of another dreamer. A Yuwipi man is referred to honorifically as Tunkašila, just as the spirits are, or he may call himself *iyeska* 'interpreter' or 'medium,' because one of his functions is to interpret the meanings of visions to others, and also to relay the instructions of spirits whom only he can see, hear, and understand.

When a man receives a vision that is interpreted to mean he must become a Yuwipi man, he often serves some years as an apprentice. But the prayers, songs, and material objects he uses in his ceremonies are his personal property, because he alone has been instructed by the spirits in their specific uses. The ritual paraphernalia are sacred and are usually burned after a Yuwipi man's death or else buried with him. In some circumstances a son who has also received a vision instructing him to "walk with the pipe," as the Yuwipi man's vocation is called, may inherit his father's paraphernalia. In rare instances a Yuwipi man may bequeath his paraphernalia to an aspiring young practitioner.

Once a man has accepted the responsibility of being a Yuwipi man, he is obliged to lead a good life and to make many sacrifices. He must pray with the pipe every day and often revitalize his power by going on a vision quest. If he did not do so his power would wane, and he might even risk losing his life or that of a loved one. Although the Yuwipi man shares a close relationship with the spirits to provide long and healthy lives for all his grandchildren—that is, all his people—he is fearful of the spirits he invokes. More than the common people, he recognizes the awesome power of the spirit world, and he understands more clearly than others the spirits' absolute power. He must do nothing that offends them: he particularly must handle the pipe properly and avoid women during their menses.

Just as a Yuwipi man fears his own powers, he may be feared or mistrusted by others, because some men communicate with the spirits for evil purposes and are capable of inflicting misfortune and sickness on the people. He must learn to contend with petty jealousies, because the common people will always be watching to make sure he conducts himself properly. If he does not, they will think his power is diminishing, and his followers will leave him for a stronger Yuwipi man.

Yuwipi men cannot charge fees for their services, though they are often accused of doing so. But Oglala standards a person does not have to pay, though he will be expected to donate something to the Yuwipi man if the service enhances his life, and he must pledge to sponsor a thanksgiving ritual within a year. If such a thanksgiving is not offered the spirits will become angry, and the person the ritual benefited will be in danger.

The Yuwipi man is particularly suited and trained by the spirits to diagnose and treat "Indian sickness," illnesses that generally were common to the Indian people before the white man arrived. If a patient is afflicted with a "white man's disease" the Yuwipi man diagnoses the illness and usually recommends that the patient be treated at the public health hospital or go to a white doctor. Some Yuwipi men have been known to consult with white physicians and the Yuwipi man may conduct a ritual in the hospital. But in any case the Yuwipi man always receives credit if the sick person recovers. If the patient has a white man's disease and does not recover, the white physician is held responsible. But if he recovers from either Indian sickness or a white man's disease, the Yuwipi man receives credit for the cure because he has properly diagnosed the case.

In addition to conducting the vision quest, sweat lodge, and Yuwipi rituals, a Yuwipi man may also be asked by the tribe to supervise the sun dance or assist the sun dance director. When there are many dancers, a number of Yuwipi men may collaborate to conduct the sun dance, and each will supervise several dancers, instructing them in their duties and piercing them on the final day. Yuwipi men may be seen talking and joking together, but underlying their amiable behavior is a strong competitiveness, encouraged by their followers, who often boast of the superiority of "their" Yuwipi men.

In general appearance Yuwipi men are no different from the common people. They have no particular badge of office except a suitcase or bag in which they keep their ritual paraphernalia, which they carry only when they are about to conduct a meeting. Even during a ritual the Yuwipi man wears nothing special, and the only difference between him and the others in attendance is that he usually removes his shirt and shoes.

But though the Yuwipi man resembles the common people superficially, he is superior to them spiritually. He alone can mediate between them and the spirit world, and he alone can cure them of Indian sickness. The common people say the Yuwipi man speaks a strange language they cannot understand—a special sacred language that he uses to communicate with the spirits. He can also understand the languages of birds and animals, and it is in particular this ability to communicate with nonhumans that sets him apart from the community.

Plenty Wolf sat with his wife and son on the shady side of his log house. Though it was late in the afternoon, the sun was still hot. A light breeze played against the four-walled tent in the backyard that served as a bedroom on hot nights.

Plenty Wolf gazed straight ahead but saw very little. His eyes teared from the glaucoma that had rendered him nearly blind; it was only a matter of time before the world would be black for him. Cars sped up and down the road, but he did not hear them, for a fall from a horse when he was twenty-eight had left him almost completely deaf. This deafness was partly responsible for his seeking out a powerful Yuwipi man named Horn Chips, who put Plenty Wolf on the hill. Here the novice had a series of visions that were interpreted to mean he should walk with the pipe. He was now sixty-six years old, and for nearly forty years he had been a Yuwipi man.

His afflictions had taken their toll, and he looked much older than his age. He was small and thin, with close-cropped graying hair. His few teeth were fragile and visible only when he grinned or coughed. Plastic-rimmed glasses teetered on his bulbous nose. Time and weather had cracked his skin and wrinkled his bony hands. He wore an oversized military shirt, Levis, and black boots scraped gray at the toes. He chain-smoked, occasionally stopping to blow off the ashes, reminiscent of the days when he had smoked Bull Durham roll-your-owns, which could not be flicked like a store-bought cigarette lest they disintegrate in one's hands.

His wife, Julie, sat next to him on a metal folding chair, a remnant of a church bazaar, probably donated by some Mormon priest. The Mormons had purchased land at the junction of the Slim Buttes Road and built a church and gymnasium. They were responsible for bringing electricity to the community. The missionaries were nice young men, all blond, who wore white shirts and ties no matter how hot the weather. They chauffered the people around the reservation, held hot dog roasts, and organized basketball and "kitten ball" games for the young people. But Julie cautioned her granddaughters and nieces, slim and beautiful teenage girls, not to "wrestle" with the Mormons. Despite their taboos against drinking, dancing, smoking, and other evils, they had a reputation for chasing young Indian girls, perhaps because of their polygynous tradition, which it was said took primacy over the other teachings of Joseph Smith.

Julie was heavyset; she wore long gingham dresses and moccasins, and usually a scarf tied gypsy style over her long silver hair. Her voice had become shrill, perhaps from shouting to make her husband understand her. As she chattered to him about the latest town gossip, it was never clear whether he even heard her. But she chirped away, her moods changing from an almost pleasant chiding of the reckless antics of the younger generation to a harangue about the neighbors' new house being too close to her yard.

Their son Basil sat on the ground Indian style, leaning against the log cabin rather like his father, gazing aimlessly into the distance, now and then combing the horizon and waiting for something, anything, to move so it could be measured and contemplated. Despite his handicaps Plenty Wolf was the first to notice the pickup coming fast toward his house, and he called his wife's attention to it by pointing with his chin. Stones flew toward both sides of the road as the truck screeched to a halt. Wayne Runs Again climbed down and stood for a moment with his hand on the gate. Plenty Wolf could not tell who it was and quietly asked his wife. She replied that it was his nephew, Runs Again's boy, but that she couldn't recall his first name. Wayne entered the gate and walked up to Plenty Wolf. "*Hau Tunkašila,*" he said. "Hau Grandfather."

This was a sign for Julie and her son to leave, for the greeting was not the conventional *Hau kola* 'Hello friend,' or Hello uncle, which would also have been proper. The ritual greeting, the use of the honorific, signaled to everyone that there was important business to be discussed between the young man and Plenty Wolf, and this should be done in private.

Wayne came closer so he could be recognized, and the old man greeted him with "*Hau Takoja,*" Hau Grandson, the appropriate ritual response. "They said you would come," he said in Lakota, and this astonished Wayne. "The spirits," Plenty Wolf added in English, and laughed a "he-he-he" not in keeping with the dignity of his vocation. But Plenty Wolf laughed often—about gossip, about his neighbors, about his relatives, and even about the spirits. Laughing and joking with or about them did not offend the spirits because they too had a sense of humor that only he fully understood.

Wayne was flustered because the old man had expected him, and he tried to explain his reason in Lakota but faltered. "*Taku* . . ." he began, "*taku* . . . I wanna . . . *taku ociciyakin kte, Tunkašila* . . . I— uh—I wanna talk to you . . . *eyaš* . . . *eyaš* . . . *inska* in . . . my dad . . . uh . . . *lila kuja* . . . I dunno."

Plenty Wolf was patient. He said, "Smoke first. *Cannunpa.*" And he fashioned his left hand to represent the bowl of a pipe and tapped it with his right hand as if he were tamping tobacco into it. The young man understood. He took a cigarette from his shirt pocket, lit it, and handed it to Plenty Wolf. Plenty Wolf took the cigarette, puffed on it, and offered the butt end to the Four Winds, the Above, the Earth, and the Spotted Eagle, with casual flicks of his wrist toward each of the cardinal points. He returned the cigarette and told Wayne to do the same. After they had smoked Plenty Wolf asked the boy what was troubling him. Wayne began to sob profusely. When he regained his composure he talked to Plenty Wolf about the agonizing pain in his father's back that came and went. He said his father was pitiful and needed help, but that he did not know what to do. He talked about his own problems too—about the drinking and carousing, and his desire to go to college, and his problem with the girl and the baby. As he talked he stopped crying and felt relief, though Plenty Wolf remained silent during the soliloquy.

When the boy had finished, Plenty Wolf took the cigarette from him, crushed it between his fingers, and threw the ashes into the wind. He told Wayne that his father was old and understood the old ways, and that he should be prayed for. Plenty Wolf was confident that he could cure the old man and could also help the boy clear his mind of the things troubling him. But he said it would require a "sing," and that the boy would have to make some kind of sacrifice to help his father through his ordeal. Plenty Wolf told Wayne he should pledge to go on the hill—Plenty Wolf would put him there—and at the same time his father should come so the people could pray for him and ask the spirits to heal him. Wayne should kill a dog and buy cloth for offerings and some groceries; there would be a feast afterward.

But first they would have a sweat. The boy would come with him into the lodge, and Plenty Wolf would pray for him and tell the spirits his intentions. The sweat would rid his body of evil and clear his mind so he would be ready to seek a vision and gain knowledge about himself.

Architecturally, the only permanent shrine in Oglala religion is the sweat lodge. It stands, sometimes wavering in the wind, in sharp contrast to the countless Christian churches that dot the reservation—little frame boxes with identical steeples and church bells that look as if they had all been constructed by a Mission Construction Company. All are painted a sacramental white and have blue- or green-shingled roofs. It is as if they had come off an assembly line, just the way the federally funded housing projects deliver prefabricated homes intact to the owner's land.

The sweat lodge is a perfect symbol for Oglala religion; when not in use the structures look rather pitiful: a dome made of willow saplings stuck into the ground, bent over, and tied in place with cloth strips or rope. There is something exceedingly profane about them when not in use, in contrast to the white man's shrines and churches, which are perpetually sacred, set off from the rest of society in a feeble attempt to separate religion from the culture's social, political, and economic institutions. The sweat lodge reflects the Oglala principle of austerity and simplicity: the entire universe is a cathedral; everything is permanently sacred unless desecrated by human foibles that cause disharmony between humans and the rest of nature.

At this time a special ritual is required to reinstate a balance among all living things, and only then are special places like the sweat lodge temporally and spatially separated from the rest of the mundane world; it is only during the ritual itself that special rules of conduct are in force and require different behavior toward nature.

When not in use, the sweat lodge becomes a playground for children, who dodge in and out of the framework, stepping into the central hole where the heated stones are placed during the ritual. It is a stopping place for multitudes of dogs, who lift their legs and declare the sacred saplings, placed there in honor of the various aspects of Wakantanka, their special territory. It is a meeting place for ants, spiders, grasshoppers, and flies seeking refuge from predatory birds who alight on the willow frame during their morning feeding. The sweat lodge is often invaded by a recalcitrant cow or a frightened horse, and it tolerates all these intrusions, along with the constant battering of the wind against its desiccated skeleton. It is partly this tolerance that makes the sweat lodge potentially sacred; like humans, it is subject to the whims of nature and must abide by its relentless impositions.

It was about four o'clock in the afternoon when Yellow Boy began throwing wood into the firepit twenty feet north of Plenty Wolf's sweat lodge. He arranged the wood in a large starlike pattern and surrounded it with the stones that had been left scattered in the ashes of a previous fire. He then piled more wood on the stones and poured on a gallon of kerosene. He lit a match, threw it on the pile, and jumped back as the flame shot up several feet before it subsided to an even-burning fire.

Wayne and his father had arrived an hour earlier, bringing the cloth they had purchased in White Clay for the tobacco offerings and flag offerings. Wayne remarked to Plenty Wolf that when he ordered the cloth at Randy's store the salesgirl said that, judging by the colors of cloth and the number of yards, it looked as if he were going to have a Yuwipi. He was a little embarrassed. Julie began the arduous task of cutting up the cloth to make the long and short strings of tobacco offerings her husband needed for the vision quest and Yuwipi.

It had taken only two days to prepare for the rituals. Wayne got credit at the local store and was able to buy meat, potatoes, bread, crackers, coffee, flour, sugar, lard, and cans of stewed tomatoes. He was instructed to obtain a pipe and, since he had no money, he went to the high school, where senior citizens had taken over a small room in the basement. A dozen of the old-timers spent their days making pipes. Large blocks of catlinite had been transported from Pipestone, Minnesota, and they used the school's power drill to make the holes in the bowls quickly. They sat around talking and smoking, filing away at the half-finished pipes. Rods of ash wood were stacked on one of the tables for the pipe stems. Business picked up in the springtime when young men would be going on vision quests or preparing for the sun dance, so they worked busily, turning out the pipes in assembly-line style. Wayne found one old man who was willing to trade a newly made pipe, a rather plain one, for a spare tire, a rim, and a jack.

As the heat of the day subtly gave way to evening, Plenty Wolf told everyone to get ready for the sweat lodge. The fire had burned down, and the stones were white-hot. Plenty Wolf led the small group of men: his son Basil, Wayne, and Plenty Wolf's son-in-law, who was a particularly good singer and knew all Plenty Wolf's songs. Old man Runs Again was too sick, he said, to go into the sweat lodge, so Plenty Wolf told him to sit outside the lodge and lean against it so the heat from inside would help his back.

Basil, with the help of Yellow Boy, who was to serve as "janitor" for the sweat lodge, began draping blankets and tarps over the sapling framework, being careful to tuck them in neatly around the outside of the base. Once these were in place, the men began to strip off their clothing, which they piled on the ground. Naked, Plenty Wolf handed his pipe to Yellow Boy, along with tobacco and matches, and stooped to crawl through the narrow doorway left open at the east end of the lodge. Each of the naked men then crawled clockwise around the central firepit. Plenty Wolf took his place on the north side of the doorway; his son-in-law followed and sat next to him. Wayne next took his place, as he had been instructed, on the west side of the lodge, at the *catku,* or place of honor, directly opposite the doorway. Basil went in last and seated himself to the south of the doorway. All sat Indian style, legs crossed in front and heels pulled close to their bodies to keep them as far as possible from the central hole. They snuggled backward against the bare willow saplings.

Yellow Boy handed in to Plenty Wolf a galvanized bucket of water and a tin drinking cup, which Plenty Wolf placed on his right a foot from the hole. Yellow Boy stood outside the lodge leaning on a pitchfork, waiting for his next instructions. Finally Plenty Wolf spoke: "*Wana!* Now!"

Yellow Boy walked over to the firepit and picked up the first large stone, which weighed almost ten pounds. Balancing it on the pitchfork, he eased it through the doorway of the lodge, carefully dropping it to the east of the hole. While he returned for another, Plenty Wolf and Basil used wooden paddles to roll the stone into the hole, leaning it against the west side. As soon as the first stone was in place the men began to mutter in wavering voices, Hau-au-au-au, ha-ha-ha-ha, hun-un-un-un, as the heat from the first stone settled on their naked bodies. Perspiration immediately broke out, and they sniffed loudly and cleared their throats. Plenty Wolf laughed a little and called for the next stone. Again he and Basil maneuvered it into the hole, resting this one against the north side. Two more stones were handed in, and they were placed against the east and then the south side of the hole until the four stones formed a base on which the other stones would rest. The heat seemed to enliven the fresh sage on which the men sat, giving them a pleasant smothering feeling. Two more stones were handed in and placed, one on top of the other, on the four-stone base. Finally a seventh stone was rolled into the hole in a rather random way. The men sat silent, perspiring and gazing into the hole, watching each step with apparent detachment. The lodge was growing hotter and hotter; their eyes began to tear, and they cleared their wracked throats more loudly as if they were trying to spit up phlegm from their lungs.

Once the seven stones were in place, with the hole only a third of the way filled, Yellow Boy brought in smaller stones, as many as he could carry with each load. The frame of willow saplings began to feel hot and the men moved slightly forward, careful not to thrust their bare knees too close to hot stones. The stones were white and dusty, and shone red through the ash covering them. The process seemed interminable, but finally all the thirty rocks were in the hole. When a slight breeze rushed through the doorway, it was as if each man except Plenty Wolf grasped part of it and sucked it into his lungs like a drowning man last breath before he sinks. Plenty Wolf, satisfied with the stones, called for Yellow Boy to close the doorway, and the lodge became dark except for tiny red eyes that peeped through the film of dust enveloping the stones.

Plenty Wolf began:

"Ho Tunkašila Wakantanka, in these dark days I sit with my relatives in the camp circle. Just as in former times we sit here and pray to you by name so that all our relations will be in good health, and nothing evil will happen to them."

The others replied in unison, "Hau!"

"Ho Tunkašila Wakantanka, today we offer you this pipe so that we may gain knowledge. And we ask you to help us, to help all of us because you are the strongest of all. Help us so we will be safe and well. To this end, we offer you this pipe."

Again the others replied, "Hau!"

Plenty Wolf continued to pray, and after each significant intention was offered the other men replied "Hau!" knowing precisely when to do so, as if they were following the libretto of an opera, knew when the score ended, and displayed their confidence by being the first in the audience to applaud.

Plenty Wolf continued with a lengthy prayer in which he asked Tunkašila Wakantanka to help the poor, the sick, young people who had relocated, and those who stayed on the reservation with nothing to do. He asked that the soldiers who had gone to fight across the water return safely, not only the Indian boys, but all the soldiers. He prayed that wars should end soon; that there be no more killing and no more mourning over relatives killed senselessly in fighting far away from sacred ground. He prayed for people to have food, money, and many children to help them when they became old and feeble. And he prayed that those who had to transact business with the federal bureaucrats would be spared red tape, the endless standing in lines and sitting in waiting rooms that was the bane of the people on the reservation.

Saying, "So that my relatives may walk in health, we offer you this pipe," Plenty Wolf ended his formal prayer. He took the tin cup and, joking that the handle was really hot, dipped the cup into the bucket and began to pour water on the heated stones.

Four times he threw water on the stones. Each time they hissed, with rushes of sibilant steam rolling up into the men's faces and causing them to sputter such meaningless phrases as he-he-he or hi-i-i-i-i and to clear their throats and nostrils and slap their bodies with their hands. As the choking steam filled the dome, Plenty Wolf's son-in-law began a song:

> I send a voice above.
> With the pipe, I send a voice above.
> "I do this because I want to live with my relations."
> Saying this over and over, I pray to Tunkašila.

The rest of the men joined in with the son-in-law, but his voice was loudest and clearest. After the first rendition he began a second, the rest again joining it. When they finished, he shouted out, "*Mitak' oyas' in!*" 'All my relations,' and each one in turn breathlessly repeated "*Ho. Mitak' oyas'in.*" Plenty Wolf quickly added the command,

"Yugan yo! Open it up!" a signal to Yellow Boy to open the doorway of the lodge. Yellow boy went into action, rolling up the tarp over the doorway. Plenty Wolf added *"Tilazatanhan! Tilazatanhan!* The back too! The back too!" And Yellow Boy ran around the lodge and rolled up the tarp on the west side.

The breeze broke through the haze like a wave, lapping over the men's dripping bodies so they whimpered with delight, Ha-ha-ha-ha. They snorted and bathed in the cool air as if they could not only feel it, but taste it and smell it and hear it beating against their slippery bodies. They rapturously rubbed the wind into their arms and chests and into their scalps, and across their faces. It was briefly pleasant and cool, but the stones in the deep hole seemed to frown at such pleasure, the embers now flickering in the intruding breeze.

Plenty Wolf dipped the cup into the water bucket and passed it to Basil, who drank almost the whole cupful, then threw the remainder onto the stones, saying *"Mitak' oyas'in."* The rest replied, *"Hau!"* They savored the water, joking about how large the stones were, and how hot. As each drank he slobbered and muttered ah! unh! in his delight. The cup, filled each time by Plenty Wolf, made the rounds of the lodge and finally was handed out to Yellow Boy, who also drank from it and said *"Mitak' oyas'in."* The cup returned to Plenty Wolf, and the men sat savoring the coolness. Then Plenty Wolf said, *"Mitak' oyas'in. Hau. Hau. Iyoĥpa yo!* Close the door!" Yellow Boy closed the west side first, then rolled down the door flap.

The smell of sage once again filled the quickly heated lodge. Perspiration immediately broke out on the men, and the coolness evaporated in the darkness. Plenty Wolf took the cup and, this time more casually, sprinkled water onto the stones. The men responded to each rush of heat with ha-ha-ha-a. He began to pray:

"Ho, Grandfather. First of all, if any of us have fallen with the pipe, forgive us. Wakantanka, in these dark days one of our common boys lives upon this earth knowing that his body is one with this earth. We know that this body comes from you, Wakantanka, and the boy knows also, and he wants to take up this pipe and give thanks to you."

The rest of the men replied, "Hau!"

"And here this common boy has a father, and his father is ill. Therefore this boy wants to do some suffering for the benefit of all his relations. Therefore he has promised to take up the pipe, and live with it hereafter. Wakantanka, on this day we thank you for this opportunity, and for everything. We ask you to listen to him and give him your guidance. Tunkašila, he wants to take up this pipe so that his relations will live, and they will be free of all temptations, from distress, and from any future troubles. So tonight this boy is going to praise you with the pipe. So help him plan his future life, and do not let him be tempted by evil. We pray that he will not be discouraged in what he does, and that he will have good thoughts toward you, and patience. Make him understand what good things are yet to come in his life. And make him come back safely from where he started. Another thing, Tunkašila, a lot of men fail at this, but help this boy succeed in what he is trying to do. And if any of his relatives here have evil thoughts, please take those thoughts away. So that this boy may understand all these good things from you, and so that he may find a prosperous future, I offer you this pipe."

The rest replied, "Hau!"

"Wakantanka, this boy has stepped farther ahead than the common people, so be good to him. And give him a good plan for his future so that he may carry on. And if it is possible that you want him to serve you, so may it be. And he will thank you for helping him, and for all these things. And so, Tunkašila Wakantanka, we pray to you this way with the pipe. So let the thunders work for you, and the Four Winds, and all the animals and things that watch over the earth. So that all of this may be, I offer you this pipe."

The rest replied, "Hau!"

Plenty Wolf, now began to beat the tin cup against the bucket and led the following song:

I pray first to Wakantanka.
I pray first to Wakantanka.
I pray first to Wakantanka so that I may
live with all my relations.

Everyone joined in the second rendition, and when the song was concluded Plenty Wolf cried out *"Mitak' oyas'in,"* everybody repeated it after him, and again he called for the door flap to be opened.

The east and west flaps were opened, and the men relished the cool breeze. Plenty Wolf called out to Yellow Boy to hand in a cigarette, and the boy lit one and passed it in to Basil. Each man dragged on the smoke a few times and said *"Mitak' oyas'in"* before passing the cigarette clockwise around the circle. They did not smoke ritually, offering the butt end to each of the cardinal points. This was just casual, pleasurable smoking. The cigarette made its way around the circle, then it was offered to Yellow Boy, who smoked it down and unceremoniously threw it away.

The respite was shorter this time. Basil asked how many more times there were—that is, how many more times the lodge would be closed—as if he had lost all track of time and ritual sequence. Plenty Wolf said there would be two more times, then told Yellow Boy to close the flaps. The sweat lodge enveloped the participants in sage and steam. Plenty Wolf continued praying:

"Tunkašila Wakantanka, all these animals that watch over the earth are my friends; that is why I am walking with this pipe. And I live a life of suffering and hardship, and I recognize that this is not an easy life. And I must watch myself with every step that I take with the pipe. So I carry this pipe with me, and I sit down here and pray with you now. May all those things that this boy prays for be granted to him. Tonight he is going to stand there alone on the hill, and we pray that he will return safely when it is over. I ask you for these things."

The rest replied, "Hau!"

Now a long silence ensued. No one prayed; they just sat in the heat and darkness. Plenty Wolf occasionally muttered "Hau!" as he talked to some spirits who had arrived and were instructing him in sacred things. He finally spoke:

"In that silence the Tunkašila have said that they see us all gathering here for this occasion, and tonight, though the boy will be standing on the hill alone, he will be protected."

Turning to Wayne, he said, "The Tunkašila will be praying for you. And if you pull through successfully you should offer up a thanksgiving ceremony. Tunkašila said that is the right way to do things, the way you are doing them now. And if there is any sickness or no matter what you ask for through the pipe, they will always answer you and give you their help if you pray this way. The Tunkašila are well pleased that you are going through this. Now in the east, there are some Indians in a tipi and they are slapping their knees and saying, 'We never realized there would still be someone approaching us in this way.' It was in the midst of these men that I came to understand the ways of the pipe. No one ever came there, they said to me, but then you came to us seeking knowledge. But you did come, and you know we are good friends. Whatever you do, don't stumble and stagger with the pipe. Don't fall or turn your back on the pipe, or evil things may happen to you. No matter what bad things might happen, they told me that I must carry on the ways of this pipe faithfully, and if I do I will continue in a righteous way."

After Plenty Wolf had finished, he told Yellow Boy to open the flaps. He did so quickly, understanding that the men were exhausted.

When the flaps were open Plenty Wolf called for the pipe. Yellow Boy removed it from the sacred hill to the east of the sweat lodge, lit it, and passed it in to Basil. Each man took the pipe and smoked it, saying *"Mitak' oyas'in"* after he had finished. The pipe went out after the second man smoked it, so Plenty Wolf asked Yellow Boy to pass in the matches. It was lighted again, and the men continued to smoke.

"This is the last time," Plenty Wolf announced after Yellow Boy had smoked the pipe outside the lodge. "Close the flaps."

Again water was poured on the stones, and the men muttered, making animal sounds as the heat enveloped their bodies. Plenty Wolf's son-in-law quickly began the last song, and with it the final stage of the sweat lodge. He sang:

> Someone who flies well makes a voice known.
> Someone who flies well makes a voice known.
> To whomever loves them and trusts in me,
> I send a voice.

After two renditions of the song, Plenty Wolf called for the flaps to be opened, and the sweat lodge ended.

The Vision Quest: On the Hill

The men crawled through the doorway of the sweat lodge like the first Lakota emerging from their subterranean womb. Their sweaty faces and bodies celebrated the cool air, and they quickly began to dry off, some using towels they had brought along, others grabbing up clumps of sage to mop away the perspiration. They were pleasantly exhausted from the ordeal, light-headed as if their next steps would let them ascend from the earth and walk through the air, over hill and mountain, just as the sacred people could do before the white men came. In the beginning this is how the Four Winds found their places. They were told to walk across the mountaintops until each came to his own home, and they traveled far until each one arrived at his place, where they still live today, waiting to be called to the aid of humans.

The men dressed quickly, except for Wayne, who was instructed to throw a star quilt around his shoulders and wait in his pickup truck. It was only moments before dusk, and on the western horizon a phalanx of stratus clouds were backlighted by rich red sun tones. Basil and Wayne's father joined the boy in the pickup, Basil sliding behind the wheel. Plenty Wolf, his wife, and his son-in-law got into the son-in-law's car. Mrs. Plenty Wolf carried the tobacco offerings she had made, neatly rolled up on a piece of pasteboard to keep them from tangling. She also carried the folded cloth squares that would serve as the flag offerings on the hill. There was a sense of urgency now, for they must reach the hill before dark. Some of the other women who had been working in the kitchen got into a third car driven by Horn Cloud, and soon the caravan was rocking down the eroded gumbo driveway to the Slim Buttes road. From there they took another gravel road that led to the base of the sacred hills two miles away.

The pickup arrived first, and the three men waited for Plenty Wolf's car before they all climbed out. The third car pulled up behind them, and soon everyone congregated at the base of the first of six adjoining hills. Mrs. Plenty Wolf handed the tobacco and flag offerings to her husband, and Basil handed his father four willow canes and the pipe bag in which Wayne's pipe had been placed. It was now time for the ascent, to be made only by Plenty Wolf and Wayne. The others leaned against their cars talking and smoking while the two began the long walk up the hill.

A slight breeze kicked up the long prairie grass, which waved now to one side, then the other as the two scuffled through it, picking their way up the trailless side of the first hill. Halfway up, the hill became steeper, and they had to clutch at withering tumbleweeds or clumps of sage to keep their balance. Their objective was the second hill, somewhat steeper than the other five, where they would find the sacred place at which many men before Wayne had pledged themselves to the Tunkašila and had lain in the vision pit as they rested during their daily and nightly rounds of prayer.

Less than half an hour of daylight was left when they reached the top and found the vision pit, which was overgrown with grass. Plenty Wolf immediately began to prepare the sacred place where the boy would stand and pray and rest for two days. On a vision quest one day is equal to the time it takes for the sun to rise and set, the second "day" being counted as the time of darkness, the lunar domain. Wayne therefore had pledged, in white man's terms, to fast and pray and cry for a vision for one full day beginning with the conclusion of the most recent sweat lodge and lasting until the next one, which would be held when he was taken off the hill the following afternoon.

Plenty Wolf quickly pulled the long grass away from the pit, revealing a trench about two feet wide by six feet long, and perhaps three feet deep, big enough for a large man to lie in. He then tied the colored cloths to the willow canes and stuck them into the crumbly earth at the four cardinal points: black for the west; red for the north; yellow for the east; and white for the south. Once the flag offerings were in place, he took the pasteboard on which the tobacco offerings were rolled and, starting at the west flag, unrolled them so that the long string stretched around all four flags, delineating a space about ten feet square. It was in this space that Wayne would stay for the duration of the vision quest, occasionally crawling into the pit to rest, but being careful not to fall asleep throughout the ordeal. The vision would come to him only when he was fully awake, praying with the pipe to the Four Directions, the Above, the Earth, the Spotted Eagle, and all the Tunkašilas who might appear to instruct him about his future, and the future of his family and other kin in the community.

Wayne stood watching Plenty Wolf. He shivered a little as a cool breeze began to blow, and Plenty Wolf told him he could crawl into the pit if it got too windy, but to come out frequently and, beginning with the west, offer the pipe to each of the directions, walking clockwise from one flag to the next until the circuit had been made. Naked except for the flimsy star quilt draped over his shoulders, Wayne told Plenty Wolf he understood. He looked out over the expanses of hills and draws that surrounded the sacred hill. It was getting late, and the yard lights around each of the community homes were coming on; soon he would see only the pinpoints of light, and the ground below him would be dark. The hills were bare where he stood, with no trees to shelter him. The sky was turning blue black, and he could look out across the land to the north where thick groves of yellow pine were silhouetted against the sky in the last few moments of dusk.

The two stood inside the sacred place, and the flags flapped in the night breeze. Plenty Wolf asked Wayne if he were ready, and the boy nodded yes. Plenty Wolf took the pipe from its bag, filled it with tobacco, and lit it. He then began the prayer on the hill:

"Ho, Tunkašila Wakantanka, before I pray, forget any of the evil things we have done in the past. I offer this pipe to you, Tunkašila Wakantanka, because this common boy here has a father who is ill—some days he is in misery, and other days he seems to regain his health. The boy wants his father to have a healthy life. The boy will lift up his voice to you and pray.

"The boy came up this hill with a healthy body, and he is happy about this and wants to thank you for his well-being. So that help will come to him from every direction, I offer you this pipe.

"Ho Tunkašila Wakantanka, we thank you for this day. The boy has prepared himself for this day, and he prays that all his friends and relations will have a peaceful life. And I join him in prayer so that nothing evil will ever happen to his family. And this boy standing here also wants to pray that he may leave some of his bad habits behind and live a good life. Therefore, Tunkašila Wakantanka, the boy wishes you to make a good plan for his future and remove any snares he might fall into. And help him do away with all those things that can hurt his body. From now on he will depend on you, and I pray with this pipe that you will give him everything he asks for."

Plenty Wolf was silent for a moment, deliberating. Then he continued:

"I pray that this boy standing here may go on to college, and that when he finishes he may make use of his education so he can live among white people and have the same knowledge they do.

"The boy has said that he would offer you the pipe in this way, and now here he is. Give him all the things he will need to get his education, so that his family can also live like white men. That is why I offer you this pipe. There are some people among us who are sick in the hospital, and I pray that they will get well during these summer months and be happy. That is why I offer this pipe to you. And also Tunkašila Wakantanka above, whom we wish to work for us and help us with knowledge. And we will pray to the Four Directions that the animals will come and be our friends. You have said it would be so, and that is why you gave me this pipe and told me to use it this way."

Plenty Wolf for a moment addressed Wayne:

"And, my boy, you are going to take this pipe, but the life you lead will not be easy. That's what the Tunkašila told me, and it was very true. Nevertheless, I carry this pipe among my people. But I fell many times. . . ."

Then, continuing, Plenty Wolf prayed:

"Therefore this boy is going to take this pipe and help me. Ho! All you animals, we come to make an offering of tobacco. And because this boy wants to walk with the pipe, I pray that all you animals help us. Tonight, watch this boy; help him. Take away any bad and evil things from him. Do not let him be tempted by evil things, or hear unkind words, or see anything that might frighten him away. All we ask is for good things, and that he will have a good vision. And we pray that he will pull through safely, and that when this is over he will return cheerfully to the place he came from. For all these things, I offer you the pipe.

"Tunkašila, we pray that all the animals watch over him, here on this sacred hill that has been made holy by means of tobacco and these other offerings. Here in the midst of these offerings to you, one will be left alone. Watch him until the end of his time. This is why I offer you this pipe."

Plenty Wolf, now concluding his prayer, handed the pipe to Wayne. He also gave him the tobacco pouch and some extra matches. The boy took the stem in both hands and held it across his chest, while Plenty Wolf gave him final instructions:

"When you feel sleepy, just lie down. If anything approaches, you will know it. And if anything tries to bother you tonight, pray to Wakantanka alone. You will know that Wakantanka exists. This pipe is just like a weapon, a firearm to be used against evil. There is nothing to be afraid of. These are the things I want to tell you. If you feel sleepy, lie on the other side. But as morning comes face the dawn, and when the morning star rises, pray to him."

Without further words or gestures, Plenty Wolf left the boy standing in the center of the sacred place, alone with the pipe, the flags, and the tobacco offerings. The old man walked down the hill in the darkness, feeling his way with his feet. A crescent moon began to rise, like a yellow watermelon rind nibbled away by a hungry ghost. The yard lights looked like fireflies, and above the stars were bright and flickering. From north to south one could plainly see the Milky Way, a gauzy, luminescent road over which walk thousands of ghosts so light and airy that they do not penetrate the trail and fall to earth.

The fluttering flags and the smell of the fresh breeze from the south made the boy who stood in the center of the universe feel that, despite what Plenty Wolf had said in his prayers, he was now entirely alone on the sacred hill. And he began to cry.

Preparing for the Sing

The three cars jostled along the bumpy gravel road passing the community dump, then veered east on the Slim Buttes road for the short way back to Plenty Wolf's home. The cars eased down through the cool draw, then turned sharply into the ascent up the gullied gumbo road. A number of other cars had arrived, and people were busy carrying blankets and tarps to the back house where the Yuwipi would be held. Two men had already begun carrying all the movable furniture out of the spare house. The cast iron stove was too heavy to budge, so they covered it with a blanket and laid some sprigs of sage on top. The spirits who would be invited to the meeting did not like white man's things, so every effort was made to remove them—particularly radios, mirrors, and items made of iron. It was also necessary to make room for everyone attending.

As furniture was being removed, other men began to nail blankets and tarps over all the windows. Both the inside and the outside of each window were draped, so the room could be made absolutely dark. Chinks in the walls were stuffed with paper and cloth to prevent even the subtlest rays of moonlight from penetrating the room and discouraging the spirits from attending.

Some exposed wires crisscrossed the corners of the room, and Horn Cloud suggested placing sage on them, since they could not be removed. He feared that some of the spirits might become mischievous, as they were prone to be, and might hang the Yuwipi man or one of the adepts by his heels from the wire. Plenty Wolf himself on one of his vision quests had been hung upside down over the side of the butte by the spirits, and it is said that such pranks were often played on other Yuwipi men in the past.

Other restrictions were placed on the adepts to ensure the success of the meeting. Women having their menstrual period were forbidden to enter the Yuwipi because they offended the spirits. One woman told how someone having her period once went into a Yuwipi. The meeting started, but soon all the covers on the windows were ripped off. The Yuwipi man told the people that there was a woman among them who was having her menses, so the spirits became frightened and returned to their homes. Everyone ate the food and then left.

Another man said that if people who disbelieve come to a Yuwipi meeting, the Yuwipi man will know it and ask them to leave. If the unbeliever does not leave, the Yuwipi man will dismiss the adepts, saying that the meeting will not work. He told of an incident in which a Yuwipi man said that no one wearing a (Catholic) medal would be permitted to stay in the meeting. One man had a rosary in his pocket but was afraid to say so. Soon something in the darkness picked him up and threw him out the window. On another occasion, a man who did not believe felt something on his lap. He put his hand down and touched something wet and hairy. He was so frightened he screamed, and the meeting had to be stopped.

The women who had been cooking in the main house now began to carry blankets, star quilts, canvas tarps, and small pillows into the back house. They distributed them around the periphery of the room, which measured about ten by twenty feet. The bedding materials were rolled up and placed against the walls for Runs Again and the other people to sit on, and enough space was left in the center for Plenty Wolf to construct the *hocoka* 'camp circle' where he and the spirits would pray throughout the meeting. A kerosene lamp was left by the doorway to give more light to the workers.

Once the room was ready, two men nailed blankets inside and outside the doorway, which was on the east wall. They held the drapes aside to let the adepts file into the room. The men entered clockwise and immediately took their seats on the south side of the room; the women filed past them and sat down on the north side. The west wall was left vacant for the singers, who entered after the rest. They passed in front of the other seated men and sat down facing the doorway. There were four of them—Horn Cloud, Brings, Elk Boy, and Red Cloud—all well-known singers from the community who were equally skillful at singing powwow songs and sacred songs.

Mrs. Plenty Wolf entered carrying an armful of flags and tobacco offerings like those she had prepared for the vision quest. For the Yuwipi, however, there were six colored flags instead of four, the additional two representing the zenith (blue) and the nadir (green). In addition to the long string of tobacco offerings, rolled around a piece of pasteboard, she carried a smaller string of thirty-three tobacco offerings used only in the Yuwipi meetings. She sat down in the northeast corner of the room in a place reserved for her and held the flags and tobacco offerings in her lap.

Behind Mrs. Plenty Wolf, Basil entered, cradling in his arms seven three-pound Butternut coffee cans half-filled with earth. Plenty Wolf followed, carrying the suitcase that contained his ritual paraphernalia. Some of his relatives explained that, though he had bought the suitcase in Chadron more than twelve years earlier, it still looked shiny and new and never seemed to show its age. This was attributed to its containing sacred articles and was also considered a reflection of Plenty Wolf's personal power. When it is not in use Plenty Wolf keeps the suitcase in a dilapidated car parked about fifty yards south of his house, where it, along with the herbal medicines he sometimes uses, will be safe from contact with menstruating women. Should any of these sacred objects be touched by a woman in this condition, or come close to her, they would lose their efficacy and Plenty Wolf would have to take them into a sweat lodge and pray for the spirits to revitalize them. Although everyone in the community knew where Plenty Wolf kept his ritual paraphernalia, there had never been a case of theft or vandalism, and this too attested to the power of the pipe and the other sacred objects as well as to the power of Plenty Wolf. The personal items of a Yuwipi man were considered particularly potent, and few would risk approaching them lest harm befall them or someone in their family.

An old woman told her own experience: When she was a child her family was getting ready to move camp. Her father asked her to pack his pipe bag and pipe in the wagon. Instead of wrapping them safely in a shawl, she simply threw them into the wagon box along

with the other bedding. The family moved and that night set up a
new camp near a wooded creek. As they unpacked the bedding the
pipe fell to the ground, and in the darkness her father stepped over
it. When he discovered his error he reprimanded his daughter,
saying that she must be more careful in how she handled the pipe
and must have more respect for it. That night the girl entered the
tent alone and was horrified to see a thin old man with white hair to
his waist sitting in the back of the tent. He pointed at her and told her
to listen to her father's advice and respect the pipe. She was so
frightened she fainted.

Basil put the cans on the floor, and Plenty Wolf began to
construct the *hocoka*. Facing west, he laid out five of the coffee cans in
a line from north to south, spaced about two feet apart. He first set in
place the west can, then the can marking the zenith, followed by the
can that would contain his personal altar, then the nadir and the
north. He then took the remaining cans and placed one in the
southeast corner of the *hocoka* representing the south, and another
in the northeast corner representing the east. Once they were in
position, he walked over to his wife and took the flag offerings,
which had been tied to thin willow canes. He placed a tobacco
offering in the corner of each flag where it was attached to the willow
cane.

Plenty Wolf thrust the butt of each flagstaff into its appropriate
can. First he placed the black flag in the west can, the red in the north
can, the yellow in the east can, and the white in the south can. He
then placed the blue flag in the zenith can and the green flag in the
nadir can. The flags secured, he opened his suitcase and began to lay
out its contents.

Removing an eighteen-inch forked willow stick from his
suitcase, he began to make his personal altar. He tied his own *tunkan*,
two eagle tail feathers, and two quilled hair strings to the fork of the
willow. To the center of the willow he affixed the tail of a black-tailed
deer. The entire willow then was placed in the center can. With all
the flags and his personal altar in place, he took out a piece of
pasteboard about twelve inches square and laid it on the floor just
east of the central can. He opened a jar containing earth from a mole
hole and dumped it gently onto the pasteboard base. Taking a small
tambourine drum from his suitcase, he tamped the mole dirt until it
formed a circular disk ten inches in diameter. Then, taking an eagle
feather from the suitcase, he smoothed the earth with delicate waves
of his hand.

This part of the *hocoka* is called the *makakagapi* 'made of earth' and later serves as a representation of the patient. Mole dirt is used because moles are members of a sacred, omniscient community of creatures endowed with knowledge of both the surface of the earth and its subterranean parts. Like ants, who push earth and stones to the surface, moles, prairie dogs, wolves, coyotes, and other burrowing animals bring clean earth from underground. This subterranean earth has not been contaminated by humans and is thus preferred for sacred rituals.

Once the *makakagapi* had been constructed, Plenty Wolf took the short string of tobacco offerings and carefully unwound it from its pasteboard card. The offerings were then laid down so they completely circumscribed the *makakagapi*, overlapping slightly where they joined at the east side. Each of these offerings was for one of the most powerful of Plenty Wolf's spirit helpers. Each is named after Inktomi, and each represents the various personalities, attributes, and behaviors of the culture hero. These are particularly potent spirit helpers, and their essence may be imparted to the *tunkan wašicun* of an initiate, after which the owner of the *tunkan* may call on them in case of danger or in any emergency. It is not known how many of these spider spirits the Yuwipi man originally owns and employs for curing, but no matter how many he begins with, his total number will decrease over time as he gives them away to new adepts. This process of divesting himself of spirit helpers to help more and more people ultimately results in the loss of the Yuwipi man's power. Eventually he has given away almost all of his major curing powers, leading to the fundamental paradox of his calling: the more people he cures, the less power he has.

When the short string was in place, with his index finger Plenty Wolf began drawing designs on the prepared mole earth. In one sweep he drew the outline of a man's head, then carefully filled in the eyes, nose, and mouth. This was the *wicite* 'face' and represented the person to be cured. After completing the face, he then drew an X under the chin representing the Four Winds (*tate topa*). To the left of the face he drew the symbol for a pope, and directly over the face, along the periphery of the earthen circle, he made three indentations representing the Morning Star (*anpo wicaȟipi*), the Sun (*anpetu wi*), and the Moon (*hanhepi wi*), to whom prayers would be offered by those attending the meeting and by the boy on the hill.

Plenty Wolf then removed four sacks of Bull Durham tobacco from his suitcase and placed them around the *makakagapi* at the southwest, northwest, southeast, and northeast quarters of the central figure. He then placed two gourd rattles, their handles crossed, near the sacks of the northeast quarter. The rattles are called *wa-gmuha* 'gourds' and reflect the materials used in an earlier genera-tion. Today, however, the rattles are made from rawhide pieces fashioned into spheres with wooden handles inserted. The pebbles inside the rattles come from anthills, and the rattles also contain small pieces of flesh offered by any adept who so chooses. This offering of flesh (*cehpi wanunyanpi*) does not occur at all Yuwipi meetings and is never required of the patient or his relatives. On occasion, however, one of the adepts who wishes to offer up inten-tions for the patient or other sick people may volunteer flesh from his or her arms. This is also done at the sun dances, where individu-als not wishing to dance may offer up prayers by giving flesh. The explanation for flesh offerings at the Yuwipi and at the sun dances is that common people do not own anything of this world except their own bodies. If they wish to propitiate Wakantanka by means of a gift, then their own body or part of it is the only reasonable thing they may offer. In the Yuwipi meeting the flesh is placed in the rattle so that it will be preserved over time and will remind the spirits of the adept's intentions and ask their ongoing aid. Thus, though the flesh may be offered only once, it comes into direct contact with the spirits who give vitality and movement to the rattles, and in doing so it generates some of the curative powers in each meeting.

When flesh is offered in a Yuwipi meeting, the supplicant stands up in the center of the *hocoka* before the Yuwipi man has actually begun the opening prayers. The supplicant takes off his shirt or rolls up his sleeve, and the Yuwipi man inserts a small steel awl into the flesh of his upper arm just far enough to catch some flesh and raise it. Holding the flesh in this position with the awl in his left hand, the Yuwipi man takes a razor blade and slices off an appropriate piece of flesh, usually about a quarter of an inch in diameter. The handle of the rattle is then slipped out of the rawhide sphere, the flesh is placed inside, and the handle is reinserted. Often the Yuwipi man will rub some medicine on the wound before the supplicant returns to his seat.

The sounds of the rattles, which will be produced by the spirits when they arrive, are analogous to the sound of thunder. Evil spirits cannot abide the sound and will quickly leave a room when they hear it. The thunder and lightning, or what are called collectively *Waki-nyan Oyate* 'Thunder-Beings,' are spirits who reside in the west. They are noisy and raucous but are generally beneficent, endowed with the ability to rid the earth of filth and evil through cleansing rains. They are accompanied by the spirits of deceased *Heyoka Kaga*, those men who chose an unnatural form of life after dreaming of lightning or thunder. They are invisible to the common people, but Plenty Wolf can see and describe them.

Basil disappeared outside for a moment and returned carrying an armful of sage, freshly picked and extremely long. One large bunch was placed in the southeast part of the *hocoka*, and a smaller bed of sage was fashioned at the west of the *makakagapi* to serve as a pillow for the sacred pipe. He then took some short sprigs of sage and moved around the room clockwise, handing each of the adepts one sprig. Each placed the sage behind his right ear, because it was well known that the spirits liked the aroma. Wearing sage behind your ear identified you as a believer, and on seeing it the spirits were sure to leave you alone. Thus, when the adepts were instructed to put the sage behind their ears so "the spirits will know you," they responded gladly because it helped alleviate the anxiety that always seemed to grip them directly before the ritual began. Although the meeting was organized to pray for an ailing person, the spirits had a reputation for being able to injure people as well as help them. Every precaution was taken to ensure that those in attendance showed only respect for the spirit helpers. In adjusting themselves to their seats along the wall, they took care to pull their knees up so their feet would not protrude into the *hocoka* once the room was darkened. They were afraid the spirits would be offended and might retaliate by kicking them or stepping on their toes, incidents that had been reported before.

As a final measure, Basil took a piece of braided sweet grass called *wacanga* and lit one end. As it began to smolder, he carried it around the room, dousing people and objects in its sacred scent. When he was finished, he snubbed it out with his boot heel and returned it to his father's suitcase. He then took a seat on the men's side of the house, while Plenty Wolf took from his suitcase a pipe bag containing the pipe and *canšasá* 'red willow' tobacco. Plenty Wolf laid the bag on the small bed of sage. He then handed a folded star quilt to Horn Cloud, who hung it on a nail alongside the doorway. Satisfied that everything was in order, Horn Cloud took two nails from his shirt pocket and, with a few deft whacks of a hammer, nailed the door to the doorjamb.

It was time to fill the pipe.

The Vision Talk

The kerosene lamp remained lit on the floor near the doorway. Its tiny flame flickered, washing the somber faces of the adepts with a yellow ochre glow. Thirty people had assembled, and only they and the sacred altar were highlighted; the rest of the room gave up its discernible shapes to the blackness. Sacred time had not yet arrived, and a few still whispered and joked; a baby sucked noisily at a nursing bottle filled with soda pop. A singer finally tapped his drum impatiently, waiting for the sing to begin. This is characteristic of singers at sacred as well as secular events. They are very much aware that no ceremony can begin without them, and once they have arrived little time elapses before they make their presence known, usually by testing the drum. The signal was taken seriously by the adepts, who immediately became solemn, squirming into more comfortable positions around the periphery of the room.

Plenty Wolf gathered up a few sprigs of sage from the altar bed and rubbed them between his hands. He removed the pipe stem and bowl from their bag and, wadding the sage in his left hand to serve as a cushion for the bowl, spit on the tip of the pipe stem and inserted it into the bowl with a twisting motion of his right hand. It is only when the bowl and stem of the pipe are joined that the pipe is powerful, and even dangerous. When not in use, the pipe is always dissembled to prevent accidents. When thus joined it is equated to a loaded gun and must be handled with acute respect for its potential.

Facing west and kneeling on both knees, Plenty Wolf again reached into the tobacco pouch and removed a pinch of *canšasǎ* between his index finger and thumb. Holding the pipe at chest level with his left hand, almost as if he were caressing it, he slowly raised his right hand, above his head, lowered it deliberately, aiming carefully, and swirled the tobacco into the bowl. He prayed:

> I pray to Wakantanka, above whom nothing exists, and who should be regarded first in all sacred things. I pray that through this pipe I may gain knowledge, and that I may live with all my relations.

The prayer was uttered rapidly and perfunctorily, giving the impression that it had been recited many times before and that the words were a formula. But it was obviously not ordinary discourse. Plenty Wolf began each phrase on an abnormally high pitch, his voice quickly cascading down, ending each canonical statement with the words . . . *slolya canunpa iyahpeuniciyape lo* 'so that we may gain knowledge, we offer you this pipe.' Here the verb "to offer" is *iyahpekiye*, which literally means 'to cause to cast out' as a fisherman casts out his line. Thus the prayers are not simply offered directly to the sacred powers of the universe but are cast out on a trajectory that ensures their reaching the powers that reside at the farthest corners of the Oglala universe.

Plenty Wolf continued filling the pipe, each time offering the pinch of tobacco with a quick gesture in the direction of the power for which it was intended:

> To *Wakinyan Oyate*, the Thunder-Beings, who live in the west and who cleanse the earth of evil and sickness. I pray to them with this pipe so that I may gain knowledge.

> To *Tatanka Oyate*, the Buffalo Nation, who live in the north, in the place of the pines, and of life, and breath, so that they may come to look upon us favorably. I pray to them with this pipe so that I may gain knowledge.

> To *Anpo Wicahpi*, the Morning Star; *Hanhepi Wi*, the Moon; and *Anpetu Wi*, the Sun, who come from the east and who change the darkness of winter into light. I pray to them with this pipe so that I may gain knowledge.

To *Wamakaškan*, the Animals, who come from the south and travel about the earth with the power to cure sickness. I pray to them with this pipe so that I may gain knowledge.

Holding tobacco between his fingers and lifting his hand toward the ceiling, he prayed:

To the Above, where somewhere between the sky and the earth, my animal helpers will come to aid me.

Offering a pinch of tobacco toward the floor, Plenty Wolf prayed:

To *Pejuta*, Medicine; *Iyan*, Rock; *Can*, Wood; and *Wowas'ake Iyuha*, All Powers, who live in the earth and give us the power to heal. I pray to them with this pipe so that I may gain knowledge.

Finally, he held the last pinch of tobacco in front of him and offered it:

To *Wanbli Gleska*, the Spotted Eagle, who is chief of *Zintkala Oyate*, the Bird Nation, who flies the highest of all the birds, and who carries our prayers to Wakantanka. I pray to him with this pipe so that I may gain knowledge.

Plenty Wolf then continued to pray, but in inaudible tones. This was a signal to the singers, who cleared their throats, then whacked their drums solidly and sang in a startling tremolo. Their high-pitched falsetto pierced the air, above the tiny clamor of the drums. They sang in unison these words of introduction that the spirits themselves had taught to Plenty Wolf in a distant vision:

Friend, Plenty Wolf, do this over here.
Friend, do this over here.
Friend, do this over here.
If you do it, whatever you want will be so.
You, Plenty Wolf, the one sitting in the center
of the camp circle, pray to Wakantanka!
If you do, whatever you want will be so.

As the singers began the second and third rendition, Plenty Wolf took another sprig of sage and placed it in the bowl of the pipe. Thus concluded, the pipe contained all the powers of the universe, the Four Winds, the Above, the Earth, and the Spotted Eagle, and Plenty Wolf was ready to begin the *hanbloglaka* 'vision talk,' a restatement of his original vision in which he was imbued with the powers of a sacred person. The vision talk was a way of presenting his credentials both to the adepts and to the spirits upon whom he would later prevail. The singing stopped, and Plenty Wolf stood up and faced west. *"Yusni yo!"* he commanded the man next to the door. "Turn off the light."

The darkness did not consume the room all at once. First the faces disappeared, but the flags demarcating the altar seemed for a moment to resist. The colors lingered briefly, and if you focused strongly on any one of them it seemed that you could still see it after everything else was hidden. Finally, everyone acquiesced to the absence of light and became acutely aware of sound: a whimper from the baby, and the mother's drawn out "ssshh"; sniffling noses, throats being cleared, and coughing—particularly unabated coughing, as if normally disgusting bodily functions were permissible because their sources were obscured. Plenty Wolf, clearing his own throat, began:

"A long time ago a horse threw me. It threw me and really cracked my head—ever since then I've been partly deaf. And it cracked some of my ribs. I began to swell up, and some people took me to the hospital at Hot Springs. I stayed there for four days, and I thought I would die from the swelling.

"I didn't have any grandchildren then. Oh, I had an older brother and an older sister, but I was there for so long and nobody came to visit me. Pretty soon, the swelling started to go down, and I knew then I would live. I got better, and I went home. But I was still weak. That's why I went to see Grandfather [a title of respect] Horn Chips, who was the leading medicine man on this reservation.

"He took me way, way out to where my family had lived for a long time in Porcupine Community to a sacred hill, and I stayed there for four days and four nights. Nobody would let me eat anything, and I thought I would surely die. But everything was all right because I had a pipe with me.

"Now out there where I stood on the hill, there were some scaffolds, the kind they used to bury people on long ago. There were also some old graves on the side of the hill. And I stood there right among them. Now on the side of the hill there was a rock platform near a small pine tree. The hill was very high, and it was there on that rock that I stood. Nothing happened until the night of the third day. I stood there near the pine, and I was wide awake—very clearheaded. I turned to get back up the hill, but I couldn't. It was clear moonlight, and I saw that the small pine tree had grown tall and I was standing on top of it. That was the way it happened: first I was standing on the rock platform, and the next thing I knew I was on top of the tree. I said, "To pray to Wakantanka is difficult." But I prayed and prayed. Pretty soon the spirits came and let me down.

"So I prayed. And I got back to the rock platform. It was still the same night when again something strange happened. Someone who was laughing loudly came to join in, I thought. But I said to myself, 'There are no women around here.' And then, there by the pine tree, this woman came and stood there. I couldn't believe it. Then she said to me: 'Why are you standing here? What do you think you're doing here?' I didn't say anything, but I grabbed the pipe right away and began praying to Wakantanka. She walked back down the hill still laughing loudly. All in all, I saw three of those women, and I was tempted by them three times. But I held onto the pipe and prayed.

"On the last night, I stood facing south and prayed for the last time, as the spirits of a stone had instructed me. As I prayed, someone seemed to be coming, making loud growling noises. But I didn't see anything. Then all of a sudden I saw that it was a spirit. I couldn't budge the pipe, and I didn't know what was happening. But I was clearheaded, and I got down and walked on my knees. Then I stopped and prayed. A voice from behind said 'That was your grandfather talking to you. Did you understand?' No, I said. Then the voice continued:

" 'You will have a ceremony. This pipe belongs to the people. Walk with them with this pipe. Be wise. Don't be with your wife during her menses. Don't slip and fall with the pipe. Don't fall asleep with it. Don't turn your back on it. If you do there will be hardships. Always walk straight with knowledge. The people now depend on you.'

"Hau, I said. Hau. Then I saw that it was a bird, a dove. There were two doves talking to me. And I repeated, Hau.

"Five years later I went back to the hill. This time a rattlesnake crawled right near my ankles, but the spirits told me not to be afraid and not to do anything. So I said, 'Whatever you are, you rattling thing, you're evil.'

"Then a large white owl appeared, flapping its wings noisily, and it seemed to be dragging a quilt. I said, 'Get out of here, there's nothing sacred here.' But I wasn't afraid; I just stood there praying.

"On the second day there was something else behind me, but I didn't care. Then a voice said that someone behind me would give me knowledge. All of a sudden a large wolf started running around, barking loudly, and it spoke to me.

" 'When you go home,' it said, 'you will use one rattle. You will use it for five years. You will give the rattle to whomever you help, whomever is sick. And then you'll have none, and you will walk in hardship.'

"So when I got home, that's what I did. I used this rattle over and over. I used it for five years.

"Five years later I returned to the hill. It was dark, and someone was talking to me. He said, 'You will have a rope for tying you up. You will have a buffalo hide, and later a quilt, a star quilt. You will have a bowstring for tying your hands.' Then he told me to go home. So I went home and gathered up all these things. And I lay in the buffalo hide."

At the simple command from Plenty Wolf, *Ho, wana!* 'Now!' the man near the door struck a wooden match and lit the kerosene lamp. The room eased back into lightness, and the adepts rubbed their eyes as if awakened from sleep. Plenty Wolf placed the pipe on the small bed of sage to the north of the *makakagapi* and sat down in the center of the *hocoka,* facing west, with his legs crossed Indian style. He asked that the light be turned out again and he began:

"Well tonight, among those who have arrived to sit in the camp circle, there is a boy standing on the hill with a pipe. So I—all of us—will pray and sing for him so that we may know how his ordeal goes, whether he is in danger, or safe.

"That boy up there is something good. His father is sick—thus this meeting so that he may recuperate—and though the one I am talking about is only a boy he wants to do this much by himself, so he is on the hill. He wants to be safe, and he wants everything to go all right. He wants whatever is wrong with his father to fade into goodness and into health. Perhaps things are not all that bad. He wants to avoid bad things. I want to also, and that is why I am praying for him.

"The boy seeks education for himself. When he finishes the twelfth grade, he wants to go on to college. That is another reason he is praying, and that is why we are praying for him. When he finishes school, he will look for work so that he can afford to go to college. We are thankful for those good things that the boy is doing on the hill. That is why we are praying for him."

At this point the devotees responded in unison, "Hau."

"Well, Tunkašila Wakantanka, dark days have arrived and settled here. First, so that you may forget that we have wronged, we offer you this pipe.

The people: "Hau."

"And so, Wakantanka, today a boy sends his voice to you because his father was confronted with evil and now sits cloaked in sickness. The boy leaves all his bodily needs behind because he knows his life depends on you. Throughout the day and night, his voice will be heard by means of this pipe. Nothing will go wrong.

"So that he may accomplish what he has set out to do, we offer you this pipe."

The people: "Hau."

"So, Tunkašila Wakantanka, watch over him through the night. Let nothing frighten him. Let nothing tempt him. Let nothing go wrong. Let no one go near him. So that he may know all that is possible for him to know, we offer this pipe to you."

The people: "Hau."

"So, Tunkašila Wakantanka, he stands there this day, this dark day, so that he can help build a bridge to brighter days. Help him so that his ordeal runs smoothly, and so that, by the time winter comes, his family and relatives will walk restored to health. And he will beseech you to eliminate the sickness of all people, and for all children to accomplish things, to get a good education, and to be healthy. Let the family of this boy make progress. We offer you this pipe so that we may gain knowledge."

The people: "Hau."

"Some of the relations here are cloaked in sickness. Moreover, there are some children in the family who are away confined to the white man's hospital. We ask this, Wakantanka, help all of them. Remember the sick, so that they may be renewed, and that they may walk again in health and happiness. We offer you this pipe so that we may gain knowledge."

The people: "Hau."

"Well, perhaps there are some relations here who have something troubling them. Perhaps they are in need of money, food, a job, advice about their families, or perhaps some have problems at the tribal office. Well if there are, Tunkašila, help them. As each day comes into sight, help each one walk with his needs fulfilled. We offer you this pipe so that we may gain knowledge."

The people: "Hau."

"And there are children scattered about the country seeking education. It is the white men who are teaching them, so for that reason the children must leave the reservation and go away to school. Help them get a good education, for in the future they will live like the white people. We offer you this pipe so that we may gain knowledge."

The people: "Hau."

"Help the boys in the service here, and those who have gone overseas to fight in the war. Some have been wounded, but do not let any more meet with bodily harm. Make them pull through; the help you give is good. See that they take care of themselves so that they will return home safely to their relations. We offer you this pipe so that we may gain knowledge."

The people: "Hau."

"And so, Wakantanka, there is no one higher than you to whom I can speak. Somewhere between this earth and the clouds there are animals I will engage to help me. The animals are at the Four Winds. Some of them are here toward the earth. Some of them guard the earth. Tunkašila, help me. In just a little while, I will be with some of them. And in a few days, things will be all right again because all over the earth, the animals will help me. We offer you this pipe so that we may gain knowledge."

The people: "Hau."

"So be it."

Calling the Spirits

The prefatory part of the sing concluded, Plenty Wolf called for the kerosene lamp to be lighted again. He removed his shoes, which he placed outside the sacred area. The full potency of this area had not yet been realized, because a small section of the tobacco offerings had been so placed that the area was not entirely closed; a small space was left between the last can of earth and the end of the string, and not until this area was completely sealed off could the sacred transformation take place.

Removing one's shoes is both an act of humility and a reaffirmation of one's Indianness. In all the sacred ceremonies the supplicant removes his shoes, sometimes all of his clothing, to reaffirm what is taught to all children: you enter the world with nothing; you leave it with nothing; and during your life on earth it is better to have nothing.

Placing his shoes outside the sacred area was Plenty Wolf's signal to Basil and Horn Cloud that the next phase of the sing was about to begin. Both men got up and rubbed their hands with sage, an act of purification. Horn Cloud took the star quilt that hung by the door and placed it on the floor of the sacred area. Both men

walked gingerly within the space so as not to disturb any of the
sacred objects. Plenty Wolf stood up, again facing west, and placed
both hands behind him. Horn Cloud took a short thong and began
to tie the fingers of Plenty Wolf's hands together. He then placed the
quilt over Plenty Wolf's head so that one corner completely hooded
his face. Two other corners were lapped across the Yuwipi man's
chest, the left corner secured under his right arm, the right corner
over his left. Horn Cloud then took from his pocket a long leather
thong, one end of which had already been fashioned into a slipknot,
and placed it over Plenty Wolf's head, securing it tightly around his
quilt-covered neck. While Basil held the quilt securely around Plenty
Wolf's body, Horn Cloud wrapped the thong round and round him
and tied seven half-hitches down his back. The end of the thong was
then knotted around the Yuwipi man's ankles. At each half-hitch,
Horn Cloud inserted a sprig of sage.

When he was thus wrapped and tied, the two men lifted Plenty
Wolf and gently placed him face down on the large bed of sage, his
head facing west. As Horn Cloud returned to his seat, Basil ex-
tended the string of tobacco offerings so it reached the can of earth
at the southeast quarter, thus sealing off the sacred area. Basil then
called for the light to be turned off. It was time for the singers to
begin the song that invited the spirits into the meeting. They began,
their loud voices again piercing the air, soon lifted even higher by
the penetrating voices of the women:

Friend, I will send a voice, so hear me.
Friend, I will send a voice, so hear me.
Friend, I will send a voice, so hear me.

In the west, I call a black stone friend.
Friend, I will send a voice, so hear me.
Friend, I will send a voice, so hear me.

In the north, I call a red stone friend.
Friend, I will send a voice, so hear me.
Friend, I will send a voice, so hear me.

In the east, I call a yellow stone friend.
Friend, I will send a voice, so hear me.
Friend, I will send a voice, so hear me.

In the south, I call a white stone friend.
Friend, I will send a voice, so hear me.
Friend, I will send a voice, so hear me.

On earth, I call a Spider friend.
Friend, I will send a voice, so hear me.
Friend, I will send a voice, so hear me.

Above, I call a Spotted Eagle friend.
Friend, I will send a voice, so hear me.
Friend, I will send a voice, so hear me.

And so the darkened room resounded first with the voices of the
singers, then with those of the other adepts. Carefully they sang the
words of these sacred songs that had been taught to Plenty Wolf in
his visions and that he in turn had taught them. Only a few of the
singers in the community knew all the songs and the proper order in
which they should be sung. Singers like Horn Cloud were required
to be at all the meetings so they could lead the others in these songs.
As the first song ended, Horn Cloud immediately began the next:

I am building a road along the side of the clouds.
Behold it!
This sacred thing that I do is important.

As the singers began the next song, their voices were interrupted by the clatter of rattles striking the floor and walls of the
darkened room. First here, then there, seemingly next to one, then
above one's head; now against the floor, now against the ceiling,
against the walls, the rattles bounded about with abandon. The
singers continued unperturbed, their voices stronger, their words
clearer:

My Tunkašila comes to see me.
My Tunkašila comes to see me.
My Tunkašila comes to see me.

Holding the old people's pipe, I send a voice.
Saying, "I will live with my relatives."
I send a voice.

The cacophony of the rattles continued, but now they moved
more deliberately as if dancing in time to the sacred music. Soon, in
the blackness of the room, tiny sparks began to appear wherever the
rattles hit the floor, like faded streaks of luminescence scampering
playfully about in the darkness. This notified the people that the
spirits had arrived and were with them in the Yuwipi meeting. The
singers sang a final song:

I send a voice upward.
I send a voice upward.
I do this so that I may live with my relations.
With the pipe, I send a voice to Wakantanka.

The song trailed off and the drums ceased. The only sound was an occasional rattle, not as violent as before, as if the spirits, like the singers and adepts, were settling down to concentrate on the matter at hand, the curing of an ailing man and the successful completion of his son's vision quest.

After some silence Plenty Wolf spoke, his voice muffled by the quilt.

"So be it."

Around the room, people waited for Plenty Wolf to begin his dialogue with the spirits. Each imagined what the spirits might look like. They knew they were little people, perhaps three feet tall, who wore breech cloths and carried miniature bows and arrows. They went barefoot, and their bodies were daubed with mud. They were Indian people who had lived generations ago, before the white man arrived, and anyone could see them in the darkness if only he would rub on his eyes a special medicine that Plenty Wolf had concocted. They could see these little people just as Plenty Wolf was seeing them, despite the darkness, but they were afraid to look; they were afraid to use Plenty Wolf's medicine.

Plenty Wolf began to speak in muffled tones. He was apparently talking with the spirits, but only he could hear them. It was his duty to interpret to the people what the spirits were saying.

"The Tunkašila knew we were doing this, so they got ready and came over here."

The people: "Hau!"

"So . . ."(Plenty Wolf suddenly stopped speaking.) "What!" (The Spirits were obviously talking to him.) "Well!" Something. (He suddenly began to agree with the spirits in inaudible tones.) "Ho! Hau!" (Slight pause.) "They say that this meeting is good. This meeting . . . whoever . . . whatever it is you want to say will be all right. And the Tunkašila will be happy to help you out."

The people: "Hau!"

"They say they are extremely pleased that the boy is standing out there on the hill."

The people: "Hau!"

And the Tunkašila say that they will watch over him out there, and help him out."

The people: "Hau!"

"And they say that they are going to pray with him."

The people: "Hau!"

"So be it."

Plenty Wolf's discourse was suddenly interrupted by his wife, who was eager to speak directly to the spirits. Her voice was loud and shrill, as if the darkness was as a barrier and she had to raise her voice so the spirits would hear her. She began:

"Ho, Tunkašila—well, Tunkašila, we who come and sit here are but common people who are to be pitied. And, Tunkašila, this boy who is standing out there on the hill is making a great sacrifice. He is fulfilling his vow to you out there, and he is suffering. Indeed, this is a great sacrifice.

"And so, Tunkašila, help this boy out. I pray that he will return safely."

Mrs. Plenty Wolf's voice now turned from pleading tones to more demanding ones. She was stern:

"And so, two of you should go and look around up there where he is standing, because we want to know how he is making out. And we want to hear that whatever he is doing up there is going all right."

"And so, Tunkašila, two of you go up there and look over him and come right back to us with a favorable report, Tunkašila."

"So be it."

Mrs. Plenty Wolf cued Runs Again to speak now if he wished. Runs Again began in a slow, deliberate way, as if unsure of what to say:

"Ho! Tunkašila, I really thank you."

The people: "Hau!"

"This meeting is like old times, Tunkašila. And I am the only one from the old generation who is still living. Long ago—a very long time ago—my father told me about these meetings. But I didn't give them much thought. But the reason I am happy now, Tunkašila, is that a boy—one of my boys—is making this sacrifice out there on the hill. He's doing it so that things will be made clear to him.

"I am glad that he stands out there with the old-timers. And because he is taking pity on me, I really thank you, Tunkašila—for everything."

The people: "Hau!"

"And no matter what happens in the future, I want my little boy to rely on you. We all will trust in you. And I will be thankful for whatever good comes of all this."

The people: "Hau!"

"There are countless things that make me happy. For some days now I have been suffering. I didn't believe in anything before now, and then something good happened to me. One of my own sons, Tunkašila, became aware of you, and there was hope. And now I feel very active again, and my flesh and my mind are filled with joy."

The people: "Hau!"

"But I wasn't like this before. Some days I was grieving. But now I am happy because I have come here."

The people: "Hau!"

"And so I say thanks. And also, in the future, if I know where they are going to have one of these meetings, I will go there and join in with them without hesitating."

The people: "Hau!"

"And also, I would like to say something—truthfully. My father used to have these meetings, long ago. When I was small I was sick and I suffered. He wanted me to grow up to be strong, and so he took one of these stones, these sacred stones, like the one I have here, and he wrapped it up in a pouch and hung it around my neck.

"And he instructed my mother not to be hard on me. But then one day she didn't heed what he had said to her, and she began to treat me badly. Then all of a sudden the stone disappeared, and only the leather pouch remained hanging around my neck.

"And that is what happened to the stone—the stone like the one some of us carry here in the house—one about the size of a piece of flesh that one offers in the Sun dance. It just disappeared because of the way my mother behaved toward me. And now it seems as if that stone were inside my back causing all this pain I have."

There was silence as Runs Again chose his words carefully.

"I should be the one making this sacrifice—not my boy. I grew up this way, but I've forgotten much. For many years things have not been clear to me, but now I have returned to these ways of the old generation. And because of my good children, my good boy who shows that he loves me by making this sacrifice, I am sincerely thankful."

The people: "Hau!"

"I give you thanks, Tunkašila."

The people: "Hau!"

"That is all I have to say, my relations."

The people: "Hau!"

"Thanks to all of you."

The people: "Hau!"

The old man finished addressing the spirits, and now it was time for others to speak. A female voice spoke:

"I want to help that boy standing up there on the hill, Tunkašila, so tomorrow, I will offer some tobacco."

The people: "Hau!"

Another woman addressed the spirits:

"Tunkašila, that boy out there wants something, Tunkašila. I've come here to pray that you pity him and talk to him, Tunkašila."

The people: "Hau!"

"Also, talk to his father, Tunkašila, so that whatever he wants will happen. Later, tomorrow, I will offer some tobacco. So may it be."

There was a pause, and Plenty Wolf asked his wife:

Is that it? Does anyone else want to speak?

And Mrs. Plenty Wolf replied:

"Yes, now they are finished. They have all finished talking. Later, Tunkašila, they will talk some more."

The sound of rattles stirring indicated to those present that two of the spirits were leaving the meeting to check on the boy on the hill as Mrs. Plenty Wolf had demanded. The singer took the cue to begin a song:

Someone who flies well is making a voice known.
Someone who flies well is making a voice known.
To whomever loves them and trusts in me, I send a voice.

Plenty Wolf then replied to the singers, "Hau! So be it."

The time passed slowly in the darkness. The people had finished making requests of the spirits, and now everyone had to wait until the two spirits transported themselves to the hilltop where the boy prayed. Singers cleared their throats for the next song, and people around the periphery of the room coughed and shifted into better positions. It was about ten minutes before the entrance of the spirits was announced by noisy rattles. Plenty Wolf began to talk in muffled tones, the only audible voice in a dialogue. He finally spoke to the people:

"Well, they say they have seen the boy. And the boy is all right. He is happy standing there. And he is making a prayer."

The people: "Hau!"

"They say there are some Tunkašila there, and they can hear the boy praying."

The people: "Hau!"

Everybody is all right. They are all together up there. Ho! There is nothing to worry about. They say things will go all right until tomorrow."

The people: "Hau!"

"So be it. They say there is nothing to fear. The animals won't let anything get inside the sacred place on the hill where the boy is standing."

The people: "Hau!"

"And they say the boy is happy standing out there. The common people here have asked that everything go all right for the boy, and your Tunkašila are praying for those of you who spoke up at this meeting."

The people: "Hau!"

"They say they are praying and, in the future, they will pray for whatever you ask. And things will be all right. And they will help anyone who makes a vow to go through with it. This is a good meeting, they say."

The people: "Hau!"

"From here on the Tunkašila will depend on the boy, they say. And in the future, the boy will walk in knowledge, and whatever he prays for will happen. Hau! Hau! So be it."

The people: "Hau!"

Here Mrs. Plenty Wolf interjected: "Are you going to say something else?"

Plenty Wolf replied: "Well, the Tunkašila went up there to the hill and this is what they have reported. When we finish, they will be with the boy tonight and tomorrow so that nothing happens to him."

The people: "Hau!"

Plenty Wolf: "So be it."

The Curing

Everyone seemed satisfied that the boy would make it through the ordeal. Plenty Wolf thus continued:

"Ho . . . tonight, some of us here have been saying good things. And we will continue to pray together. We will put these prayers through the pipe, and we will all drink water together and pray for all mankind. So be it."

He signaled with a simple "Ho!" for the singers to begin the next song:

> I send a voice here and there.
> I send a voice here and there.
> To whom shall I send a voice?
> Tunkašila, what do you say?
> I send a voice here and there.
> Who will help me?
> Tunkašila, what do you say?

The singers sequed immediately to another song:

> It is me.
> I am sending a voice clearly.
> Tunkašila told me to do so.

It is me.

I am clearly sending a voice.

The singers finished, and Plenty Wolf addressed them: "Hau! So be it. The Tunkašila have heard your songs and they are pleased."

The people: "Hau!"

"They are praying in those sacred hills."

The people: "Hau!"

"The Tunkašila are going to pray for all of you while they are up there. Hau! . . . Hau! . . . Hau!"

These interjections were directed to the spirits, who must have told Plenty Wolf they were getting hungry and that it was time to begin the special songs sung before a dog feast. The kettle or "pot" dance, as it is called, was closely associated with the *Heyoka Kaga,* and during the ceremony dancers danced around the kettle of dog meat, thrusting their bare hands into the boiling water. Since the spirits were also *Heyoka,* they would now demand that the singers perform the *Heyoka* songs, and they, in the darkness, would perform the kettle dance around the pot of dog meat. The singers thus began with the traditional opening prayer of the kettle dance ceremony:

Wakantanka pity me.

Wakantanka pity me.

Pity me.

I do this so that I may live.

During this song, the spirits crouched in a circle around the pot, lifting first their left hands, then their right, then both hands in supplication to Wakantanka. The next song began:

They are standing at home around the clouds.

They are standing at home around the clouds.

Those Thunder People are standing at home.

They are standing at home around the clouds.

Those Thunder People are standing at home.

During this part of the song, the spirits danced around the kettle single file, following the leader, thrusting their arms into the boiling water and exclaiming that is was cold, as *Heyoka* do. This was a special song, sung only for the spirits; during a kettle dance performed by the living, a different song would have been used. After the circling-the-kettle song, the singers now sang the music for the last part of the dance, in which select members of the dancing group would charge at the kettle brandishing forked sticks and attempt to skewer the choice morsels of meat. The singers began the lively song:

> They are eating dog over here.
> They are eating dog over here.
> In the west, the Thunder People are eating dog.
> They are eating dog.
> Sacredly they are eating.

The dance was now over, and Plenty Wolf addressed the singers:

"Hau! So be it. The Tunkasila have heard your songs and they are happy. They will now help the sick. Hau! So be it. Ho . . .now another song . . ."

The singers responded:

> They make known a voice.
> They make known a voice.
> They make known a voice from above.
> They make known a voice.
> They make known a voice from above.
> They make known a voice.
> They make known a voice from above.
> They make known a voice.
> They make known a voice from above.
> They make known a voice.

The singers immediately segued into a lively dance song for the benefit of the spirits. It was a current Omaha dance, or war dance song, and contained no words, only meaningless syllables. After four renditions of the song the spirits had been appeased, and it was time for the curing ritual to begin. Mrs. Plenty Wolf, for the benefit of Runs Again and some other newcomers, explained what the patients should do.

"Stand up," she said. "Stand up and grab the flag closest to you. Grab the flag, then turn around and face the wall."

There was an immediate response from the singers, who tapped their drums in preparation for the curing songs. There was also a response from the spirits: the rattles had again come to life, chattering softly in the center of the sacred area.

The curing takes place in darkness; no one can witness it except the patient. It is a subjective experience effected by the most powerful of human spirits who control the movements of the rattles. Not only the primary patient may stand up to be cured; others who have similar symptoms may elect to be cured and may make their wishes known to the Tunkašila through the Yuwipi man. When more than one wishes to be cured, each reaches out in front of him and gropes in the darkness until he can grab one of the flags. Holding onto the flags, they all rise, without crossing into the sacred area, and turn around to face the wall.

If the patient is afflicted with pain, he or she makes it known to the Yuwipi man during the preceding segment of the sing in which those adepts who so desire declare their intentions to the Tunkašila. If someone fails to say what part of the body is affected, the Yuwipi man will ask where the pain is after the patient has risen and stands awaiting the cure.

It is during this portion of the sing that the Yuwipi man calls upon the most powerful of his helpers, those who are well versed in curing human sickness. Some of these spirits communicate verbally with the patient, whispering in his ear in a high-pitched voice. Customarily, they ask him how he feels, or where the pain is, but they may also joke with him. The spirits most frequently talk in Lakota, but some of them also speak English. A typical converstion with a bilingual spirit in the process of curing:

Spirit: *Niwašte he?* [Are you well?]
Patient: *Hiya!* [No!]
Spirit: *Niwašte he?*
Patient: *Hiya!*
Spirit: Are you OK?
Patient: No!

Only the person being cured can hear the spirit talking, because at the same time the singers are singing and drumming. In some cases, however, the spirit may speak before the curing has officially begun, and all may hear. The speech is normally in Lakota and is usually jocular, including such statements as:

"Gee, I wish I had some buffalo meat."
"I'm really thirsty. Does anyone have a beer?"
"I think I want to change my name [to a white man's name]."

All these statements elicit laughter from the adepts, who admit they like it when the spirits are entertaining.

The patients in position, the singers now began a lively song, while the rattles joined in the rhythm, dancing in time with the music:

> They come dancing. Behold!
> They come dancing. Behold!
> They come dancing. Behold!
> From the Four Winds, the stones come dancing.
> They come dancing. Behold!

As the patient stands facing the wall, he is approached by the dancing rattles. They dance near his feet, then over his head, and dart about. Soon they come very close to his head, decreasing in volume until they are barely audible. Meanwhile the singing continues loudly, the renditions being repeated over and over to allow the time needed to cure the patient. Eventually the patient experiences a touch. Something not quite discernible makes contact with his hair, then presses against his head. It touches his head very gently in a number of places, then moves to the back of his neck, across his shoulders, down his spine. Often there is an odor of sweet grass, known to be the aroma of spirits; it passes before his face and into his nostrils. Sometimes he feels wind pressing against his head, a fanning motion across his face. The touching may be repeated or may simply dissipate. Once the contact has been made, the spirits return to their violent dancing, and the rattles clatter about the room until the songs come to a close. The patient is then instructed to resume his seat.

The singers segued into another lively song, in the same tempo as before:

> Friend, I give these to you.
> Come and get them!

They were telling the spirits that the elaborate tobacco offerings had been made especially for them and were there on the floor for their taking. Having once been human, the spirits still liked their tobacco; they could smoke it later in the west where they had their home.

Plenty Wolf interrupted: "Hau! So be it."

The singers began another song:

> I have accomplished these things well.
> With the pipe of the Spotted Eagle.
> I have accomplished these things well.

The rattles danced vigorously, emitting sparks along their paths. Quickly they danced along the rectangular line of tobacco offerings, accepting the gifts from the people as they made ready to leave the meeting and return to their homes. Stamping along the floor one by one, the spirits picked up their tobacco offerings, and one by one they left. The singers once again raised a song:

> They stand at home and make a voice known.
> They stand at home and make a voice known.
> Because of your Tunkašila's influence, I give you these.

The singing ended, and there was no more sound of rattles. The luminescence had disappeared, and all was quiet in the stern darkness. Plenty Wolf spoke:

"Well, the Tunkašila will concentrate on the boy now. And they say for you to think of him too."

The people: "Hau!"

"Pray for him. And remember everything you say in your prayers, and they will help him. And tomorrow you will join in again."

The people: "Hau!"

"So be it. Turn the light on."

A different scene emerged in the pale light. The order of the altar had given way to chaos, as if the spirits had gleefully overturned the sacred space, trampling on hallowed relics, disrupting the very area that had been so carefully constructed for their edification. Sacks of Bull Durham were strewn about. The rattles were scattered. And the sacred disk of mole earth on which the face of the patient had been painstakingly drawn, along with other symbols designed to attract the most efficacious of powers, was scratched into indecipherable marks. Sage was strewn across the once-neat floor, and in the midst of this mischief sat a tired, sweating figure: Plenty Wolf.

He sat meditating, gazing into the shallow space before him. The quilt that had constrained him was folded neatly by his side, and on top of it was the thong that had bound his hands and the longer one that had bound his body in the quilt. Next to the quilt lay the long string of tobacco offerings, neatly rolled into a perfect sphere, a perfect *yuwipi*. He finally looked up at the people and said with a grin, "It's really stuffy in here." People laughed and now began to stretch their legs.

Plenty Wolf took the pipe from its bed of sage and lit it. He puffed on it a few times, praying silently, then got up and handed it to the man seated to the south of the doorway. The man puffed, said *"Mitak' oyas'in"* 'All my relations,' and passed it to his left. All the people responded, "Hau!" Each person likewise took the pipe, smoked it, and repeated *"Mitak' oyas'in."* When the pipe reached the woman with the baby, she smoked it and then laid the stem across the baby's head, repeating the sacred formula. After all had finished, the pipe was returned to Plenty Wolf, who dissembled it and placed it in the pipe bag.

Basil and Horn Cloud began to remove the drape covering the doorway, to make way for the women to fetch the food that had been prepared in the main house. Plenty Wolf began gathering his paraphernalia and putting it away in his suitcase. The mole dirt he carefully poured back into the jar, and the sage he gathered up to return to the elements. Plenty Wolf's wife collected the flags and began to untie them from their willow rods. The cloth itself would later to given to Runs Again with instructions to find some woman to cut it up and make a star quilt out of it. This cloth was regarded as sacred, and after it was fashioned into a quilt it would be particularly efficacious as a shawl to be used in conjunction with inhalants. One suffering from a cold should burn the medicine called "big root" while holding such a shawl over his head. The ball of tobacco offerings would also be given to Runs Again with instructions to keep it for good luck. The tobacco offerings represented all the living species that associate with mankind, and they were still sacred even though their essence had been taken away to be smoked by the spirit helpers.

After packing up his things, Plenty Wolf went over to talk to Runs Again. Runs Again told the Yuwipi man that his pain was gone and he felt better. He was glad he had returned to the old ways, and he promised he would offer up another meeting next year. The others sat in their places while Basil picked up the last few sprigs of sage and cleaned the floor. He then took the bowl of water and offered it to a man sitting to the south of the doorway. The man accepted the bowl and drank from it. After drinking he said "*Mitak' oyas'in*" 'All my relations,' and passed the bowl to his left. All responded "Hau!" Each person likewise took the bowl of water and drank from it, passing it clockwise and repeating the formula "*Mitak' oyas'in*" after drinking. After all had partaken of the water, the bowl was returned to Basil, who stood in the center of the floor. He looked at the bowl and muttered that he wished people had drunk more, because it was his responsibility to finish it off. Someone quipped that if it were wine he would have no trouble downing it, and everyone laughed. Basil took a deep breath and began to drink the remainder of the water. By so doing he affirmed the Oglala principle that, if nourishment is on hand, it should be consumed, for there might come a time when no food and drink are available, and the people might suffer. After finishing it he said *"Mitak' oyas'in"* and placed the bowl near the doorway. All responded "Hau!"

Some of the women had left to bring the food from the main house. The rest of the people sat around smoking and talking about the events of the week. An old man was chided for falling asleep in the meeting; he was reminded of the old saying that if you fell asleep when you weren't supposed to you would surely be struck by lightning. The old man nodded, saying he knew the story, and commenced to roll a cigarette. The baby, awakened by the light and the commotion of people talking, grabbed for its nursing bottle of soda pop.

The Feast

Another kerosene lamp was brought into the room. Women began to carry in pots and pans filled with food that had been cooked while the meeting was in progress. People who had been casually sitting about smoking now reached into paper sacks and produced a variety of ceramic and tin plates, bowls and cups, and silverware. Everyone was ready for the feast that traditionally followed every Yuwipi meeting.

The food was placed in the center of the floor, once the location of the sacred altar. Three of the women busied themselves distributing the food to the adepts. Moving clockwise, they ladled out the traditional *wahanpi* 'beef soup' fortified with potatoes, wild turnips, and tomatoes, made thin so it would go around several times. More food was always prepared than could possibly be eaten by those in attendance at Oglala gatherings. It was expected that people would bring their *wateca* buckets, usually lard cans that could hold healthy portions of food to be taken home after the meeting. Although the term *wateca* is normally glossed "leftovers," it is based on the root for "new things," and the leftovers frequently serve as staple meals over the next day or two. One is always reminded before any gathering, sacred or secular, to bring one's *wateca* bucket. It appears that this is more than customary; people who attend many feasts, particularly during the summer, can accumulate enough *wateca* to feed them over the ensuing days. It is not considered greedy to bring along more than one *wateca* bucket or to carry a cloth sack in which "leftover" pieces of fried bread can be stored for future meals. People sometimes live from one feast to the next, and carrying food home is regarded not as gluttony but as pragmatism.

Perhaps all peoples judge the success of social gatherings by the quantity and variety of food served. The Oglalas are no different. The food is paid for by the sponsor of the Yuwipi , but its preparation is entrusted to those women, and in some cases men, who know best how to prepare what is perceived to be traditional Oglala food. The most highly relished food, from the standpoint of tradition, is dog meat, particularly from a young puppy. Although repugnant to the white man and many other Indian tribes, dog has been a delicacy for the Oglalas as long as anyone can remember. A newcomer to the reservation community is often shocked to discover that the Indians keep dogs not as man's best friend, but as man's best meal—at least by Oglala standards. It is not without some ritual that the flesh of a puppy reaches the serving plate. According to a custom whose meaning had been lost, puppies should not shed blood before being eaten, so they are ritually strangled, usually by two women who place nooses around the dog's neck and pull from opposite directions. The whole carcass is then placed directly on an open fire, or on an iron grating over a pit fire, and the hair is singed off. The dog is then butchered, and the edible portions, including most of the internal organs and the head, are placed in a pot and boiled. The head is considered the choicest part, and during the kettle dance—a ritual always performed when dog meat is served—one of the objectives of the dancers is to spear the head from the caldron during the finale of the dance. In the old days the "spear man" who successfully came up with the head had the honor of presenting it to the most distinguished, and usually oldest, member of the group. Today dog meat is served still first to the older guests at a meeting, people who would be disappointed not to receive any, since it is now served only on special occasions.

At the feast for Runs Again, the dog meat was the first food served, and the portions did not quite make the rounds of all the participants. Plenty Wolf and Runs Again were served first, then the old man who had dozed through most of the meeting, and then randomly those who were next oldest.

Next to dog meat, *wahanpi,* beef soup or stew, is relished most. Today it is made with beef except on those special occasions, usually sun dances, when one or two buffalo are sent down to Pine Ridge from the Wind Cave National Monument game preserve in the Black Hills. Despite the substitution of beef for buffalo, the soup is regarded as traditional and is perhaps the favorite food for "dinner" (the noon meal) and "supper" (the evening meal). At large feasts the *wahanpi* is usually cooked in ten-gallon caldrons over an open pit fire, but for Yuwipis it is cooked indoors on a wood or gas stove in family-size pots. It is served in bowls and eaten with spoons, or sometimes with the fingers, since it contains large pieces of meat that have been cut (usually at the butcher shop) bite size.

A separate bowl is usually reserved for *wojapi,* which is made from chokecherries or wild plums boiled and thickened with flour. It has the consistency of oatmeal and is very sweet. It is not regarded as a dessert, and it often constitutes the staple part of a meal along with fried bread and coffee. After the chokecherries have ripened in late July and August, a supply of them is dried and put away. They are easily reconstituted in boiling water and provide a nutritious food over the long winter.

After ladling out the soup and *wojapi,* one woman made the rounds distributing various breads. Perhaps the most favored is fried bread, called *wigli un kagapi* 'made with grease.' The dough is shaped into triangles about the size of Danish pastries and deep fried in grease until golden brown and puffy. A second traditional bread is called "sourdough" in English and *kabubu* in Lakota. *Kabubu* means to pound together, referring to the action of shaping the dough, which is usually fashioned into a circle an inch or two thick, to fit the bottom of a frying pan. Along with these traditional breads there are huge quantities of store-bought bread, which the Lakota call *tacangu aguyapi* 'lung' bread because of its spongy consistency, and boxes of saltine crackers. Each person receives a slice or two of bread and a handful of crackers, placed on top of their soup bowl or *wojapi* bowl.

One woman disappeared and soon returned with a large enamelware pot of steaming coffee, wearing gloves to avoid burning herself. The coffee, black and presugared to an almost syrupy consistency, was made in traditional "Indian" or "cowboy" style, the ground coffee added directly to the water and boiled.

The distribution of food took about fifteen minutes, but people began to eat as soon as they received their shares. The women continued making clockwise rounds, distributing second helpings to be placed in the *wateca* buckets. By the time a third round began, most people had finished their first helpings, and more food was loaded into their empty bowls until all the serving pots were empty and returned to the kitchen. A woman brought in a box of sweet rolls, exclaiming that she had almost forgotten them, and these were quickly distributed two at a time. As each person finished the meal, he or she lit a cigarette and leaned back against the wall, waiting for the rest to finish. People now discussed common things—the weather, horses, cows, the tribal office, white people—or commented on the meeting, usually in a joking manner, noting how one of the spirits stepped on someone's feet because they were too close to the sacred part of the floor, or how another spirit came so near a man could feel the wind on his face; or how another person thought a rattle was going to hit him in the head, it came so close during the sing.

And so people talked and ate. When the last one had finished eating, Basil nodded to the man still sitting at the south side of the door, and the man began, *"Mitak' oyas'in"*. Everyone responded, "Hau!" Each person in succession, clockwise around the room, repeated the formula and received the response, thus officially ending the Yuwipi.

While the women picked up the last of the cooking pots and utensils, some of the men took down the blankets and tarps that covered the windows. Others began to bring back the furniture that had been removed.

Outside the air was clear and cool, and the stars stood out magnificently against the blue black sky. A wisp of a cloud crossed the moon, and the Milky Way charted its course across the southern sky. Somebody complained that his pickup would not start, and a young boy was summoned to get a set of jumper cables from Basil's car. Engines turned over, and the children playing around the bare framework of the sweat lodge were called home. A few embers still burned in the firepit where the stones had been heated, like a final comment on the auspiciousness of the sing.

In the west, the sacred hills were silhouetted against the night sky. Plenty Wolf carried his shiny suitcase out to the abandoned car and locked it in. He casually gazed out over the hills and craned his neck to look back toward the west. He muttered something about being happy it would not rain that night and said he would have to be up before dawn to prepare for taking the boy off the hill.

The Vision Quest: Off the Hill

Wayne did not clearly understand it. He was not sure whether the vision had come during the night or in the first glimmer of dawn. But it had come—easily, he thought. It just appeared, far out ahead of him, where moments before there had been emptiness. He was surprised it had happened so easily. He was amazed it had happened at all.

He had followed Plenty Wolf's instructions, but he thought that, though he was sleepy, it would have been impossible to fall asleep. If nothing else, the south wind had blown strongly all night. At first he was afraid it might be a tornado blowing up from the southwest, but then he recognized it as only a summer wind. It was familiar from a time he had camped out and made the mistake of pitching his tent so the doorway faced south. All night the south wind had blown steadily, with a force he thought would surely carry the tent away. But early in the morning, just like this morning, it had died down, subsiding in the early morning sun.

The south wind was warm, and all night it made the flag offerings hum and whirl and crack against themselves with reports like firecrackers. The incessant flapping kept him from dozing off. He thought it sounded like thousands of giant rattlesnakes quivering their tails in unison, or like a summer hailstorm clattering on the cabin roof.

But this morning the flag offerings hung limp after their nocturnal bout with the wind. Overhead the sky was clear and blue, where he thought there had been clouds before. But, again, he could not be sure when it was cloudy. He remembered the picture, painted in watercolors whose pigments ran when struck by the rain or melting hailstones, mingling so that primary colors mixed into secondary and tertiary ones. Then they all fused until things were dark and mysterious, as they had been before.

He had followed Plenty Wolf's instructions assiduously. He rose frequently from the pit, moving first to the west, then to the north, then to the east, and then to the south, always ending by facing the strong, warming wind. It blew the tears across his cheeks and down his neck, till his hair seemed heavy on his back from the weight of his own tears. And he prayed to each direction:

> *Wakantanka unšimala ye.*
> *Miyakuye ob wani kta ca lecamun we.*
> Wakantanka pity me.
> I want to live with all my relations, that is why I am doing this.

Soon the flapping of the flags was overpowered by another sound, this time like reverberating drums—heavy thuds very near him. He clutched the pipe, the firearm that would protect him from danger, and dared not look behind him, where the drums pounded so loudly he thought his eardrums would break. To his amazement, the sound was now coming from the sides, and soon he could hear it directly in front. He was frightened, but he clung desperately to the pipe as if it were a rope thrown to a drowning man. He looked at the ground, expecting to see a tormented ocean beckoning him to jump in. Instead he saw at his feet tiny black ants scampering busily around their anthill, working relentlessly to push little stones from under the ground onto the top of the hill. As the ants walked, their feet pounded the ground with drumlike sounds that seemed to shake the earth. They tramped about, pushing boulders in front of them; occasionally they would tire and lose their grip so that the boulders tumbled back into the abyss like a landslide that gains momentum with a deafening sound like thunder. The ants were frantic, their footsteps racing now this way, now that way, trying to retrieve the boulders they had worked so hard to push to the top of their world. Each step was more agonizing than the last, thudding and echoing against the earth's surface, as if it were stretched taut over some subterranean resonator, a drum shaped by the universe itself.

Wayne finally cried out:

Ho Tunkašila Wakantanka omakiya po!
Ho Tunkašila Wakantanka, help me, all of you help me!

The ants stopped, as if they had been commanded, and Wayne tried to follow them with his eyes as they disappeared into the tiny funellike hole like a black stream of syrup sucked into the earth. Everything was motionless but the flag offerings, still driven in an erratic cadence by the south wind.

Wayne had stopped crying. Exhausted, he crawled back into the pit. Here in the seclusion he could hear his stomach rumbling. He had not eaten for how long? It seemed like days, and hunger stabbed at his insides. His mouth was parched, and his tongue stuck to his palate, choking him. He tried to make his saliva flow, but his thick tongue remained paralyzed in his mouth. Perhaps he would die. He prayed that he would not, and in desperation he wiped his palms against his sweaty face and body and licked the perspiration off them like a dog lapping water. The moisture tasted salty and good, and for the moment he was relieved.

Wayne could not help imagining how much he was like the ants that had scurried to the safety of their hole at the command of the Tunkašila. The earth was cool and soft against his body, and he smelled the grass and sod around him as he had never done before. He thought of other things that might be in the pit with him—insects, spiders, worms, all crawling things. But he was not frightened because he was not only with them, but one of them, and things beneath the earth would do no harm because they were sacred.

He thought how much the vision pit was like a grave, a white man's burial place. People often joked about going to your grave on the vision quest. But it was only a joke, and he did not dwell on the thought; he was not frightened about being "buried" because he could see the moon and stars overhead, clear and consoling. Soon his hunger and thirst left him, and he remembered the pipe he had been clasping so tightly that his hands had begun to ache. He feared he could not release the pipe if he wanted to, and then he became afraid to try. The more he thought about the pipe, the tighter his grip became, as if he might smash it between his fingers. At this moment the stem of the pipe began to move and wriggle in his hands as if he were holding a snake, moist and scaly, and he could feel the stem, or the snake, breathing—inhaling and exhaling in his hands by means of its sinewy muscles. He was afraid to look at it because perhaps it really was a snake, a rattlesnake that would suddenly quiver its tail, mimicking the death rattle of a human. He was afraid that if he looked at the bowl of the pipe he would see a terrifying sight, huge fangs bared, and red puffy eyes as large and uneven as the stones in the sweat lodge, all steamy and oozy, staring back at him. He broke out in a cold sweat that seemed to transform the earth around him into muddy gumbo, and he feared that the pit would disintegrate beneath him so he would sink and drown in a muddy pool while all the crawling things watched and could not help him because he could not say the words—Tunkašila, Tunkašila, Tunkašila. . . .

He jumped out of the hole clutching the pipe and fell toward the west flag. He was so tired he could not stand, so he crawled to the flag offering and held on to it, caressing it, wiping the black cotton cloth on his face. He wanted to wrap himself up in it, and he begged the west wind to help him. He cried out to the Thunder-Beings to rid him of filth and evil and to purge the rottenness inside his body and his mind. As he fumbled for matches to light the pipe, the wind began to blow even more strongly from his left, and every time he struck a match the wind blew it out. Then he realized that the south wind had stopped beating against his flag offerings, and everything about him was still except some sourceless wind that erupted like a devil duster every time he lit a match, preventing him from smoking the sacred pipe. In a panic, he managed to pull himself to his knees, and from this position he cried out with tears streaming down his cheeks and chest: Pity me. Pity me. Pity me. At this moment he saw a tremendous cloud in the west where before there had been nothing but a peaceful blue black sky and a crescent moon retreating across the diaphonous ghost road.

The cloud formation was the largest he had ever seen, and he felt obliged to stand up and pay it respect. His body was no longer weary; he felt tranquil, serene. He knew this was a sacred sight; it was so still, like puffy white smoke rather than a cloud. The formation was edged with a thin black line, like a caricature of a cloud rather than a real one. The line had been drawn neatly by a steady hand, on a parchment of periwinkle hues, and hung in the sky by an invisible hand for him alone to praise.

The more he gazed at the cloud the more it seemed that it could move. Yes, it did move slightly toward him. Then he thought he could control its movement by looking away from it. And he was right. Whenever he gazed intently at it, it moved slightly toward him. But when he took his eyes off it, it stopped. He wondered how long this game could continue, and he laughed a little over his ability to control this wonder. But as he laughed the thin line that had set the cloud off from its blue background began to grow thicker and thicker. It was now transformed from a pencil line to a less discrete wavy line like one painted with a brush. Its ebony blackness began to wash away into grayish hues, melting into the puffiness like wax heated by the rays of the sun, first loosening a little, then beginning to run into all the layers and grooves and channels of the cloud formation. The whole monolith began to glow unevenly like a huge luminescent globe, becoming more defined and detailed until he saw that the light was not the soft glow of a firefly, but sharp, forked, and silvery. He knew then that it was lightning jabbing at the cottonlike clouds, causing them to bulge a little, then slowly change their shape, as if someone were rolling a giant snowball right at him. It grew as it came closer, now billowy and gray, raucous and clamoring. Lightning shot out in all directions, each fusillade of sparks followed by booming rounds of thunder, reverberating against the land so it shook violently. The boy thought he would fall as the hill trembled, and he moved his foot to the side, then to the front, then to the back to keep his balance.

He was afraid the tremors would shake the pipe out of his hands, and he remembered in desperation Plenty Wolf's admonition that the pipe was his weapon against evil, a firearm that would protect him from all harm. In a sudden rush of courage he thrust the stem of the pipe at the onrushing clouds, holding it tightly, and began to sing:

I am building a road alongside the clouds.
Behold it!
This sacred thing is important.

As he sang over and over these words that had come to him spontaneously, the tumultuous cloud formation seemed to divide in half just at the point where he was aiming the pipe. And between these clouds he could see multitudes of Thunder-Beings, gargantuan forms riding giant horses. Their faces were hidden in the clouds, but he could see their bodies, painted with zigzag symbols of the lightning. Each held long leashes of lightning fastened around the necks of slaves, humans who had dared to ignore the teachings of the Tunkašila and so after death were driven by their thundermasters across the celestial plains.

The thunder became mixed with the sound of the giant horses' hooves. The boy held even more tightly to his pipe and prayed to Wakantanka that he might live with all his relations, now more confident and courageous because the pipe was indeed protecting him so that nothing, not even the cataclysm before him, could bring him harm. The Thunder-Beings galloped by, their slaves screaming unintelligible phrases as the cloud split and the cacophonous hordes rode past on either side, leaving him the vision of a sacred road directly before him that led to infinity through a peaceful periwinkle sky. All was quiet except for birds singing: first a meadowlark encouraging him to be brave, then a host of swallows chirping above him in their clipped language, which he could not understand but still rejoiced in. The meadowlark told him to go home. Then it turned and with its characteristic pecking movement sauntered down the hill. As it moved farther away, its footsteps sounded human, as if it were wearing boots and trudging through the tall prairie grass. At this moment Wayne recognized Plenty Wolf coming over the hill.

The sacred space was a shambles; the flags had been knocked over, and Plenty Wolf began to gather them up and to roll up the tobacco offerings. Wayne was tired, and he blinked his eyes, which smarted from the sun and dust. Plenty Wolf looked at him and the pit and laughed his he-he-he laugh. He took the pipe and helped the boy adjust the muddy star quilt around his shoulders. Then he took him by the arm, and the two walked slowly down the hill.

At the bottom about twenty people had gathered, some who had been at the Yuwipi and others who had heard that someone was being taken off the hill and were curious to watch. When they reached the bottom Plenty Wolf took the pipe, filled it with tobacco, and began to pray:

"Ho Tunkašila Wakantanka, all the relations and friends here thank you and offer you this pipe. There are some other people here who also thank you in our prayers for this boy's success.

"Tunkašila, this boy now has fulfilled his promise to you. So may all his relations live a long life, and may they all live happily in this world. This is why I offer you this pipe."

Some of the people responded, "Hau!" And they all got into cars to go back to Plenty Wolf's house.

The Sweat Lodge: Outside

Runs Again now felt well enough to join his son, Plenty Wolf, Basil, and Plenty Wolf's son-in-law in the final sweat lodge. By the time they reached Plenty Wolf's house, Yellow Boy had already built a large fire and the stones were turning white-hot. It was about seven o'clock in the evening when the five men stripped off their clothing and crawled into the lodge.

Yellow Boy took the pipe Plenty Wolf had filled and capped with sage and placed it on the sacred hill east of the lodge so the bowl rested at the base of the mound and the stem leaned diagonally against the mound and pointed west. Then, taking his pitchfork, he picked up a large stone and eased it through the doorway, where Plenty Wolf and Basil rolled it into the hole and placed it in its proper position. The first seven stones were thus arranged as they had been in the first sweat lodge. Yellow Boy labored with the remaining stones, then handed in the bucket of water and the cup. At Plenty Wolf's command, he rolled down the door flap and secured the tarps and blankets around the entire base of the lodge.

As the sweat lodge proceeded, Yellow Boy sat on his haunches near the doorway. He was tired from lifting the heavy stones, so he rested and smoked a cigarette. The sun was still warm, and he wiped beads of perspiration from his forehead. Inside the lodge, he could hear the muffled tones of the praying and singing, and the hiss each time water was dipped onto the stones. Although he was outside the lodge, he was an integral part of the ritual, for it was his duty not only to open and close the flaps during the intermissions, but to turn the pipe so that its stem faced the proper direction each time the door flap closed.

Plenty Wolf called for the door to be opened, and Yellow Boy jumped up and hurriedly raised the front and back flaps. The men were drinking water inside, and when the cup came back to Plenty Wolf he handed it out to Yellow Boy, who drank some and said *"Mitak' oyas'in."* The men inside replied with the familiar "Hau!" He passed the cup back in to Plenty Wolf, and after a short time he closed the flaps again and moved the pipe stem so it pointed to the north.

And so the sweat lodge continued. During the second respite, Yellow Boy repeated his actions, but this time he was asked to light a cigarette and pass it in. The cigarette made the clockwise round of the lodge and was then passed out to him. He smoked it and threw it away. He then closed the flap and moved the pipe so it pointed east. He heard Plenty Wolf pray:

"Ho Tunkašila Wakantanka, this boy has made a promise and has fulfilled it. From the sweat lodge he departed, and now he has returned. Therefore, Wakantanka, grant him and his family a good life. And if there is any more sickness in his family, I pray to you to help them, and in that way the family will walk happily. This is why I offer you this pipe."

The others responded, "Hau!"

"Wakantanka, continue to hear this boy's prayers and answer them, and if you do he will offer up thanks to you in the years to come. This is why I offer you this pipe!"

The others responded, "Hau!"

"And here look favorably upon us who are in need and help us, especially those who are sick somewhere. Cure them of their sickness and give all of us a healthy life. Those are the things we ask, especially now in the summer. This is why I offer you this pipe."

The others responded, "Hau!"

"Ho Tunkašila Wakantanka, help all our relations with those daily needs—money, food, jobs, business transactions—especially those who are having difficulty accomplishing things. Help us and give us all these things so we may thank you in our prayers. And that is why I offer you this pipe in this way."

The others: "Hau!"

There was some silence, and Plenty Wolf repeated over and over, "Hau! . . . Hau! . . . Hau! . . ." as he listened to the spirits talk to him. He then addressed the others, saying, "The Tunkašila say all of you should pray that the boy's prayers will continue to be heard, and, if so, he will walk joyously." And the men replied, "Hau!"

Addressing the boy, Plenty Wolf said, "Your Tunkašila are praying among those hills, and they will continue to pray for you. Beware at all times, and always pray to the Tunkašila." The boy replied, "Hau!"

Then, continuing, Plenty Wolf prayed:

"So hear all of our prayers, Tunkašila, and remember us. And Tunkašila, wherever there are common people who are sick and suffering or are in danger, protect them and help them regain their health."

Then, addressing the boy, he said, "Well, this is it. And from now on, this is the way you should pray." Then, as if he were witnessing something in the darkness, something sacred being revealed to him that no one else could see or hear, Plenty Wolf began:

"In the easterly direction there is a tepee, and it is painted red. Inside there are three men slapping their knees as if they are surprised. They are shaking their heads, and they are saying, 'We never thought this boy would make it, but through the help of the Tunkašila he did pull through, and he recognized that these Tunkašila are his friends. So take this common pipe, and go forth with it. This is the common pipe that you will walk with through your life. Boy, be always alert! Even though you might walk and stumble, or stub your toe, or even fall down, or even try to turn back with the pipe, be careful or something bad will happen to you.' "

Plenty Wolf then concluded:

"Therefore always be alert, and all those things you ask for yourself and your friends will be granted. That is why I offer this pipe. And whatever we embark upon in the future, may we have a healthy life, may our daily needs be fulfilled, and may we always be safe from harm. In this way we offer you the pipe."

Everyone responded, "Hau!" Plenty Wolf asked Yellow Boy to open the flap and pass in the pipe. He took it off the sacred hill, lit it, and handed it to Basil. After each had smoked the pipe, he said *"Mitak' oyas'in,"* and finally it was handed outside to Yellow Boy, who

smoked it and repeated *"Mitak' oyas'in."* He then returned it to the
sacred hill, pointing the stem to the south.

When the flap was closed, the men sang:

> I send a voice above.
> With the pipe I send a voice above.
> "I do this because I want to live with my relations."
> Saying this over and over, I pray to Tunkašila.

The sweat lodge was now over, and Yellow Boy opened the door
flap. Led by Plenty Wolf, the five men crawled outside, once again
entering the mundane world.

Before Wayne and his father left, Plenty Wolf instructed them
that they must offer up a thanksgiving ceremony to the spirits within
the year so that the Tunkašila would continue to help them. If they
did not, the spirits might become angry at their lack of respect, and
harm might befall them. Plenty Wolf gave Wayne the tobacco offerings he had prayed with on the hill, and he gave the old man the
tobacco offerings that were rolled up at the Yuwipi. He also gave
them the flag offerings and instructed them to have them made into
a star quilt.

All the men shook hands; Plenty Wolf went to the abandoned
car near his house and placed in the back seat his suitcase with all its
sacred contents. His wife walked to the side of the house, pulled the
tarps and blankets off the framework of the sweat lodge, and hung
them on the clothesline to dry. It was dark now and the sacred rites
were completed, fulfilled. The people returned to their everyday
world, and were it not for the glow of the heated stones, still breathing laboriously in the earth inside the sweat lodge, it might have been
just another common day.

Postlude

"I'll keep you bound
Both hand and foot, in savage custody."
—"Whene'er I please, a god will set me free."
I think he meant; I'll die. For death is final.

Horace

When I last saw Plenty Wolf in 1971, he told me about a number of misfortunes that had befallen him. His wife Julie had died, and he was inconsolable. She was truly his helper in both a spiritual and a practical sense. It had become more difficult for him to see and hear, and she increasingly served as his eyes and ears as the years wore on. With her dead, Plenty Wolf experienced a loneliness that the other members of the family could not assuage. But he was not totally helpless. He still walked along the dusty road to Pine Ridge to shop or to talk to other old-timers who sat all day on the street corners just—looking on, as the Indians say.

About the time he lost his wife, another misfortune occurred that he could explain only as the act of some mischievous Inktomi, walking around the universe looking for an unfortunate person to play a prank on. He had apparently found Plenty Wolf, and he had caused Plenty Wolf to lose some of his most important ritual objects—his last two rattles. It was the loss of his rattles that made Plenty Wolf decide he could no longer conduct Yuwipis.

With sadness he told me in Lakota about these hardships, but after relating each incident he gave a slight chuckle that under-

99

scored how helpless humans are against the wishes of the spirits. The superhuman beings and powers that live in the west had given him his vision, and now they had decided to take it away. It was no use to go on other vision quests or into other sweat lodges. Plenty Wolf was old, and he knew—as all the others in the community knew—that he had lost his power. He would never approach the hill again.

As if losing his wife and his vision were not enough, shortly thereafter his son-in-law, the husband of his oldest daughter, died. Another part of his vision was thus ripped away, because his son-in-law was Plenty Wolf's chief singer. Plenty Wolf had taught him all the sacred songs he had learned on the hill, and the younger man faithfully attended all his father-in-law's Yuwipis to lead the rest of the people in the songs.

Plenty Wolf looked at me through the milky veils covering his eyes and told me that none of the people in the community came to see him anymore, except his children and grandchildren. He had heard that those who needed advice or the proper ceremony when something was bothering them now turned to a Yuwipi man from another community. It was with surprise, if not irony, that I saw Yuwipi in a fuller context. It was neither the patient nor the medicine man who really counted in the rhythmic flow of rituals. It was the people—the community, the Oglalas. Everything and everyone else was expendable. Just as the patient was cured by destroying the sacred altar, so the symbolic death of the Yuwipi man, wrapped at once in the swaddling cloth of birth and the shroud of death, guaranteed the symbolic life of the patient. But it was the people who really prospered and persisted. The shamans and patients as individuals, were unimportant.

Another death followed. Plenty Wolf's *unmahetun* 'co-parent-in-law,' his daughter's husband's mother, died, one of the last of the real old-timers who could remember moving camp by horse and travois. And after she died her son was bludgeoned nearly to death in his own house by a drunken intruder.

Plenty Wolf was old and tired. He had walked with the pipe, and just as the spirits had promised him in his first vision, when he stood among the scaffolds of the dead and heard the midnight voices speak for the first time, his whole life had been hard.

Not long after I returned home, I learned by telephone that a roving band of youngsters had dragged Plenty Wolf out of his son's pickup truck one evening and had beaten him severely. He recovered, but soon thereafter he fell ill and had to be taken to the public health hospital. He lay there for two weeks, then died.

Plenty Wolf was buried at Holy Rosary Mission with full Catholic rites, one of the odd inconsistencies that befall Yuwipi men. But, then, someone has to own the cemeteries. Before the priest could pronounce the last words over the open grave, some people in the Red Cloud Community sensed that Plenty Wolf's spirit was still nearby. Was it that fresh aroma of sage in the Yuwipi? Or was it that white-haired man smoking a pipe that somebody saw on the road last night? Ho Tunkašila.

Mitak' oyas'in

Bibliography

Boas, Franz, and John R. Swanton. 1911. "Siouan." In *Handbook of North American Indian Languages*, Bulletin of the Bureau of American Ethnology, no. 40, part 1. Washington, D.C.: Government Printing Office.

Brown, Joseph Epes. 1954. *The Sacred Pipe*. Norman: University of Oklahoma Press.

Buechel, Eugene. 1924. *Bible History in Teton Sioux*. New York: Benziger Brothers.

———. 1939. *Grammer of Lakota*. Saint Louis: John S. Swift.

———. 1970. *Lakota-English Dictionary*. Pine Ridge, S.Dak.: Red Cloud Indian School.

———. 1978. *Lakota Tales and Texts*. Edited by Paul Manhart. Pine Ridge, S.Dak.: Red Cloud Indian School.

Cooper, John M. 1944. "The Shaking Tent Rite among the Plains and Forest Algonquians." *Primitive Man* 17: 60–84.

Deloria, Ella C. 1932. *Dakota Texts*. New York: G. E. Steckert.

———. N.d. Dakota Commentary on Walker's Texts. Manuscript deposited at the American Philosophical Society, Philadelphia.

Densmore, Frances. 1910. *Chippewa Music*. Bulletin of the Bureau of American Ethnology, no. 45. Washington, D.C.: Government Printing Office.

———. 1918. *Teton Sioux Music*. Bulletin of the Bureau of American Ethnology, no. 61. Washington, D.C.: Government Printing Office.

————. 1932. *Menominee Music.* Bulletin of the Bureau of American Ethnology, no. 102. Washington, D.C.: Government Printing Office.

Dorsey, J. Owen. 1894. *A Study of Siouan Cults.* Eleventh Annual Report, Bureau of American Ethnology. Washington, D.C.: Government Printing Office.

Erdoes, Richard. 1972. *The Sun Dance People.* New York: Alfred A. Knopf.

Feraca, Stephen E. 1961. "The Yuwipi Cult of the Oglala and Sicangu Teton Sioux." *Plains Anthropologist* 6:155–63.

————. 1962. "The Teton Sioux Eagle Medicine Cult." *American Indian Tradition* 8(5):195–96.

————. 1963. *Wakinyan: Contemporary Teton Dakota Religion.* Browning, Mont.: Museum of the Plains Indian.

————. 1966. "The Political Status of the Early Bands and Modern Communities of the Oglala Dakota." (W. H. Over) *Museum News* 27:1–2.

Feraca, Stephen E., and James H. Howard. 1963. "The Identity and Demography of the Dakota or Sioux Tribe." *Plains Anthropologist*, vol. 8, no. 20.

Fire, John [Lame Deer], and Richard Erdoes. 1972. *Lame Deer: Seeker of Visions.* New York: Simon and Schuster.

Fletcher, Alice C. 1884. *The Elk Mystery or Festival of the Ogallala.* Peabody Museum Report, vols. 3–4. Cambridge: Peabody Museum.

Fugle, E. 1966. "The Nature and Function of the Lakota Night Cult." (W. H. Over) *Museum News*, vol. 27, nos. 3–4.

Hassrick, Royal B. 1964. *The Sioux: Life and Customs of a Warrior Society.* Norman: University of Oklahoma Press.

Hinman, E. 1930–31. Hinman Interviews. Manuscripts deposited at the Nebraska State Historical Society.

Howard, James H. 1954. "The Dakota Heyoka Cult." *Scientific Monthly* 78(4):254–58.

Hurt, Wesley R. 1960. "A Yuwipi Ceremony at Pine Ridge." *Plains Anthropologist* 5(10):48–52.

————. 1961. "Correction on Yuwipi Color Symbolism." *Plains Anthropologist* 6(11):43.

Hurt, Wesley R., and James H. Howard. 1952. "A Dakota Conjuring Ceremony." *Southwestern Journal of Anthropology* 8(3):28–29.

Hyde, George E. 1937. *Red Cloud's Folk.* Norman: University of Oklahoma Press.

————. 1956. *A Sioux Chronicle.* Norman: University of Oklahoma Press.

————. 1961. *Spotted Tail's Folk.* Norman: University of Oklahoma Press.

Kemnitzer, Luis. 1968. "Yuwipi: A Modern Day Healing Ritual." Ph.D. diss., University of Pennsylvania.

————. 1970. "The Cultural Provenience of Objects Used in Yuwipi: A Modern Teton Dakota Healing Ritual." *Ethnos* (Stockholm), vol. 1, no. 4.

————. 1976. "Structure, Content, and Cultural Meaning of Yuwipi: A Modern Lakota Healing Ritual." *American Ethnologist* 3(2):261–80.

Lévi-Strauss, Claude. 1963. "The Effectiveness of Symbols." In *Structural Anthropology.* Garden City: Doubleday.

———. 1966. *The Savage Mind*. Chicago: University of Chicago Press.

Lowie, Robert H. 1913. *Dance Associations of the Eastern Dakota*. Anthropological Papers, vol. 11, part 2. New York: American Museum of Natural History.

———. 1954. *Indians of the Plains*. Garden City, N.Y.: Doubleday.

Lynd, J. W. 1864. *Religion of the Dakotas*. Minnesota Historical Society Collections for 1864. Saint Paul.

Macgregor, Gordon H. 1946. *Warriors without Weapons*. Chicago: University of Chicago Press.

Mails, Thomas E. 1978. *Sun Dancing at Rosebud and Pine Ridge*. Sioux Falls, S. Dak.: Augustana College.

———. 1979. *Fools Crow*. Garden City, N.Y.: Doubleday.

Malan, Vernon D., and Clinton Jesser. 1959. *The Dakota Indian Religion*. Rural Sociology Department Bulletin 473. Brookings: South Dakota State College.

Mooney, James. 1965. *Ghost Dance Religion and the Sioux Outbreak*. Chicago: University of Chicago Press.

Neihardt, John G. 1961. *Black Elk Speaks*. Lincoln: University of Nebraska Press.

Neill, E. D. 1872. *Dakota Land and Dakota Life*. Minnesota Historical Society Collections for 1872. Saint Paul.

Nurge, Ethel. 1964. "The Sioux Sun Dance in 1962." *Proclamations of the Thirty-sixth Congress of Americanists* 3:102–14.

Olson, James. 1965. *Red Cloud and the Sioux Problem*. Lincoln: University of Nebraska Press.

Pine Ridge Research Bulletin. 1968. "Wanblee Community." In *Pine Ridge Research Bulletin*, no. 5, pp. 24–51. Pine Ridge, S. Dak.: U.S. Public Health Service.

Pond, G. H. 1867. *Dakota Superstitions*. Minnesota Historical Society Collection for 1867. Saint Paul.

Powers, William K. 1961. "Contemporary Music and Dance of the Western Sioux." *American Indian Tradition* 7(5):158–65.

———. 1968. "Contemporary Oglala Music and Dance: Pan-Indianism versus Pan-Tetonism." *Ethnomusicology* 12(3):352–72.

———. 1969. *Indians of the Northern Plains*. New York: G.P. Putnam's Sons.

———. 1970. "Contemporary Oglala Music and Dance: Pan-Indianism versus Pan-Tetonism." In *The Modern Sioux*, In Ethel Nurge. Lincoln: University of Nebraska Press.

———. 1971. "Yuwipi Music in Cultural Context." Masters thesis, Wesleyan University, Middletown, Conn.

———. 1977. *Oglala Religion*. Lincoln: University of Nebraska Press.

Ray, Verne F. 1941. "Historic Backgrounds of the Conjuring Complex in the Plateau and the Plains." In *Language, Culture and Personality: Essays in Memory of Edward Sapir*, ed. Leslie Spier. Menasha, Wis.: American Anthropological Association.

Ricker, E. S. 1906-7. The Ricker Tablets. Manuscripts deposited at the Nebraska State Historical Society.

Riggs, S. R. 1869. *Tah-Koo Wah-Kan; or, The Gospel among the Dakotas*. Boston: Congregational Sabbath School and Publishing Company.

———. 1890. *A Dakota-English Dictionary*. Contributions to North American Ethnology, vol. 7. Washington, D.C.: Government Printing Office.

———. 1893. *Dakota Grammar, Texts and Ethnography*. Contributions to North American Ethnology, vol. 9. Washington, D.C.: Government Printing Office.

Ruby, Robert H. 1955. *The Oglala Sioux: Warriors in Transition*. New York: Vantage Press.

Smith, J. L. 1967. "A Short History of the Sacred Calf Pipe in the Teton Dakota." (W. H. Over) *Museum News*, vol. 28, nos. 7–8.

Standing Bear, Luther. 1933. *Land of the Spotted Eagle*. Boston: Houghton Mifflin.

Steinmetz, Paul B. 1980. *Pipe, Bible and Peyote among the Oglala Lakota: A Study in Religious Identity*. Motala (Sweden): Borgstrons Trysten.

Theisz, R. D., ed. 1975. *Buckskin Tokens: Contemporary Oral Narratives of the Lakota*. Rosebud, S. Dak.: Sinte Gleska College.

Utley, Robert M. 1963. *The Last Days of the Sioux Nation*. New Haven: Yale University Press.

Walker, James R. 1917. *The Sun Dance and Other Ceremonies of the Oglala Division of the Teton Dakota*. Anthropological Papers, vol. 16, part 2. New York: American Museum of Natural History.

———. 1980. *Lakota Belief and Ritual*. Edited by Raymond J. DeMallie and Elaine A. Jahner. Lincoln: University of Nebraska Press.

Wallace, Anthony F. C. 1966. *Religion: An Anthropological View*. New York: Random House.

Wallis, W. D. 1947. *The Canadian Dakota*. New York: American Museum of Natural History.

Wissler, Clark. 1907. "Some Dakota Myths." *Journal of American Folklore* 20:195–206.

———. 1912. *Societies and Ceremonial Associations in the Oglala Division of Teton Dakota*. Anthropological Papers, vol. 11, part 1. New York: American Museum of Natural History.

Glossary and Index
of Lakota Terms

Subject Index

Above, the, 38, 50, 62
Allen, 22
animals, 56, 57, 62
  in Oglala religion, 28, 67, 89–90
  in vision quest, 64–65
anthropology, 1–3
Ashley, Joe, 13

Bad Faces, 22
Batesland, 22
Big Road, Mark, 13
Bird Nation, 62
Black Buffalo Woman, 9
Black Horse, 10, 11, 12
Brings, 55
Brules, 8
Buffalo Nation, 61
Bureau of Indian Affairs, 31
Buzzard Butte, 11

catlinite, 30, 41
Cherokee, 19
Cheyenne River, 19
Chips, Charles, 13
Chips, Ellis, 13
Chips, Godfrey, 13
Chips, Phillip, 13
Christianity
  beliefs about guardian spirits in, 27
  and Yuwipi rituals, 6, 14, 39, 54
Cody, Iron Eyes, 18–19
color symbolism, 30, 50, 55, 56
Community Action Programs, 18
Crazy Horse, 8–10
Crows, 9

curing ritual
  description of, 65–67, 78–80
  preparation for, 40–41, 57–58
  spirits at, 71–75, 77–78, 87
Cut-offs, 22

Dakotas (Canadian), 6
disease
  treatment of, 35–36, 82
  See also curing ritual

Eagle Nest Butte, 10, 11, 12
earth, the, 29, 38, 50, 62
Elk Boy, 55

federal government
  "civilization" programs of, 22–23, 31
  prayers for relief from, 42
  suppresses Oglala religion, 7–8, 12
Fills the Pipe, Zona, 21, 22
flags
  at curing ritual, 78, 79
  ritual use of, 30, 40, 49
  at vision quest, 50, 52, 88–89, 91
  at Yuwipi, 55, 56, 63
Flesh, George, 13
flesh offerings, 58
Fools Crow, Frank, 13
Four Directions, 50, 51
Four Winds, 29, 38, 48, 57, 62, 67
Fuller, Gerald, 6

Great Spirit, 12, 23
  See also Wakantanka

Hisle, 22

Author Index